Passion At Work

Passion At Work

Six Secrets for Personal Success

Kevin Thomson

CAPSTONE

First Published 1998 by
Capstone Publishing Limited
Oxford Centre for Innovation
Mill Street
Oxford OX2 0JX
United Kingdom
http://www.capstone.co.uk

British Library Cataloguing in Publication Data
A CIP catalogue record for this book is available from the British Library

ISBN 1-900961-61-X

Typeset in 10/14 pt New Baskerville by
Sparks Computer Solutions, Oxford
http://www.sparks.co.uk
Printed and bound by
T.J. International Ltd, Padstow, Cornwall

This book is printed on acid-free paper

CONTENTS

Part 3   The Passion Pack   169

ABOUT THE AUTHOR

Kevin Thomson has pioneered internal marketing and organizational communication for more than a decade. He is Chairman of The Marketing & Communication Agency Ltd (MCA), the first European internal marketing and communication consulting firm. He has an extensive marketing and operational background in a wide range of industries including finance, leisure, manufacturing, retail, catering and consulting.

The leading authority on applying external marketing concepts internally, Thomson has developed strategies and processes that have proven highly effective in blue-chip organizations in the private and not-for-profit sectors. His approach enables companies to meet and exceed their objectives through their own people, by generating commitment and enthusiasm for business goals. He has earned the prestigious standing of Accredited Business Communicator from the

International Association of Business Communicators (IABC) and is currently President-Elect of IABC UK.

A dynamic speaker, Thomson has addressed international conferences and seminars hosted by organizations such as the Chartered Institute of Marketing, Business Intelligence, the Institute of Personnel and Development, IABC and The International Quality and Productivity Centre. He has facilitated corporate conferences and workshops for companies such as KPMG, British Airways, SAAB, Oracle, Ernst & Young, Novell, ICI Paints and many others.

Thomson has published numerous articles and is author of several management books including *The Employee Revolution* and *Managing Your Internal Customers* – the first books of their kind on the subject of internal marketing and communication. He also contributed to the chapter on internal marketing in the *Financial Times Handbook of Management,* which brings together the latest thinking from the world's top management gurus in one volume. His latest book (the sister to this one) *Emotional Capital* explores the relationships between hearts and minds and lasting business results.

To find out more about Kevin Thomson or MCA (The Marketing and Communication Agency), call MCA's UK headquarters on +44(0) 1628 473217.

To add your voice, thoughts and feelings on the subject of emotional capital, and contribute to developing the concept and that of internal marketing in the future visit the Web site at www.mca-group.com

MY THANKS

Your passion built a great business and won us awards

To three special ladies

I'd like to dedicate this book to the three very special ladies in my life – my wife Kathy Thomson also known at work as Kathy Whitwell the co-founder and driving force of our business who helps bring my ideas to fruition; my daughter Eleanor, who makes it all worth while and not forgetting my mother Jean. Each of them bring me joy and helped me to learn my male way of doing things isn't always right! I will continue to learn but to me that is what life is about.

To our 'test market'

A special thank you to Linda Jones, Communication Manager of British Airways, Jonathan Nash, Sales and Marketing Director of SAAB GB, Linda Cole, former Marketing Director of BET Catering Services and Debra Butcher, Internal Communication Manager of Royal Mail Streamline (now a team member of MCA). Also to Nicki Knowles-Leak our nanny who loves the ideas in *Passion At Work* and is forever trying to work out how to get the kids to 'do as you are told'! Their enthusiasm (among the many other clients and their colleagues we talked to – it is called research) for the concept of this book, prompted it to be written.

The team at MCA (The Marketing and Communication Agency in Marlow-on-Thames)

Thanks for putting up with a Yellow Squiggle and bringing to the party all your own ways of working. Their passion has led us to break brand new ground over the last decade, and be recognized as 'the first in internal marketing', with a host of wonderful clients, successful projects, awards, books, articles, press coverage, conferences, strategies, processes, skills, training programs and a lot more. Thanks to Liz Young, the newest and youngest member of the MCA team whose passion for teaching and training others to communicate led her to help edit this book in her own time; Andrea Schüller for project managing me; Monique Baudouin for making the layout look good.

Our clients

Thanks for your part in building our relationships and giving us the opportunity of creating a new approach to helping people and business help themselves through improved internal marketing and communication.

The second part of the book contains one of our concepts developed by our team in many leading organizations over the last ten years. The 'WHY' concept was pioneered in the 1980s and was featured in *The Employee Revolution* (FT Pitman). It was put to great use in the beginnings of one of the first Intranet developments for Bass Brewers in the UK by IBM, which went on to win a Europe Africa Gold Quill Award from the IABC – International Association of Business Communicators.

Our suppliers

Thanks to the team at the Marlow Agency. They channelled their passion for design into the original graphics for the Passion At Work concept. This design went on to be tested with SAAB at an internal event of team building and communication. This event 'Beyond The Conventional Convention' (a theme which integrates external marketing) also went on to win a Gold Quill Award for Europe and Africa.

Our publisher

To Mark Allin at Capstone, who has been so passionate about both *Passion At Work* and *Emotional Capital* he decided to publish both – together! To Tom Fryer at Sparks for a great layout. And thanks to Liz Simpson – a great editor and passionate communicator.

To you

Thank you for investing your time and energy; and money too. My goal is to make sure you are repaid – many times over!

Passion At Work: what will this book give you?

What this book is all about?

Passion At Work is all about improving communication between individuals, teams, departments and companies.

This book covers three critical areas of communication based on some fundamental principles of marketing.

- **Understanding** how you and other people think and react to what's around you.
- **Researching** how you and others communicate with each other, whether in groups or individually.
- **How to** use this information to influence others and get their 'buy-in' to what you want to put across.

How you benefit

- You'll get 'buy-in' – from colleagues, teams and whole organizations to your messages.
- You'll understand the impact of people's personalities, gender, culture, language and 'hooks' on the messages you send.

You will gain most by ...

... reading the book in bite sized chunks. Read a chapter at a time, think about it, try out the ideas. Have some fun! We shouldn't take life too seriously.

PART 1

INTRODUCTION TO PASSION AT WORK

A New Way of Communicating and Understanding People

Introducing you to passion at work

What is this Introduction about?

This introduction raises the whole issue of why we need passion at work. It begins to uncover how best to release it through the understanding of people and the teams they comprise. It then shows how everyone will become a communicator of change and will need a new set of skills.

How you benefit – the hooks

This introduction will give you a taste for the passion that can be aroused in yourself and others. You will begin to see how passion can be harnessed for both business and your own personal benefit.

You will gain most by ...

... looking upon this introduction as a section to simply 'get you in the mood' for a lot of the passion that is going to come in the rest of the book.

PASSION AT WORK

What has passion got to do with work and the way we communicate?

When we are first attracted to someone, it often doesn't matter too much what we say when we let the passion flow. As long as it is with as much emotion as possible our partner will be happy, often ecstatic.

One of the strongest emotions of all is PASSION. It is a motivator which drives us to incredible limits.

In a fulfilling relationship, physical passion is only a small part of what makes a partnership successful. In a stormy relationship the time spent arguing about passion and physical problems indicates a symptom, not the cause.

The problems we may have with passion usually go well beyond the physical. They are largely caused by our ability – or lack of ability – to communicate.

When two people know how to communicate well, they spend 10% of their time together sorting out the odd problem or two. They spend the other 90% talking, listening, laughing, joking and enjoying the good things in life. Otherwise it's the reverse!

> **"**
> *When you get right down to it, it is our ability to communicate that makes us human*
> **"**

In a strong relationship it is the passion for the ordinary things in life, jointly shared, that become the focus of the relationship.

Recognition is slowly dawning on society that we are facing a communication problem. If communication is the root cause of the negative emotions between people, then resolving this issue will allow everyone to enjoy the positive emotional feelings we can get when we react with others.

The BIG, BIG, BIG challenge in business today

"
I can't even get excited about work, never mind passionate!
"

A recent survey revealed that poor communication at work, just like poor communication at home, causes more upset, stress, loss of time, energy, motivation and morale than any other single factor in our everyday business lives.

What's more, it is killing off the one thing that most organizations need more than any other single emotion in the workplace today – PASSION.

What is 'passion at work' and how does it link with our personal relationships?

When the passion is gone, people either quit from believing in their jobs and go, or even worse, they 'quit' and stay.

We're left with people with no enthusiasm or excitement for what they do. People who have it stand out a mile. You can see it in the way they work and behave; even more uplifting is when you can see the smile on their face, or the joy of a job well done.

Passion is the rarest of commodities. Yet we can find it by the bucket load, in ourselves and in others, if only we knew where to look. This book is your guide.

Watch out everyone else if your competitors have recognized the future lies in this unique sustainable competitive advantage called passion.

The benefits of having passion at work:

- Excellence in all aspects of customer service
- Increased sales – the top line
- Increased productivity
- Huge enthusiasm for producing quality products
- People hell bent on creating and innovating great new ideas
- Drive to cutting costs
- Common goal of being the best
- Love of sharing best practices
- Great spirit in launching new products and services
- Everyone focused on adding shareholder value – the bottom line
- Motivated people producing products and services that sell!

Jot down what you would get from lots more passion in your working life

_____

_____

_____

_____

_____

All of these benefits to having passion at work add up to one thing; profitable relationships – for everyone.

The definition of a new way of doing things

This book helps you create a new way of working. It is about helping you to find the passion inside yourself and others. How? By applying the learning from a number of disciplines, including psychology, human resources, total quality and marketing and communication, and rolling them into one.

We call it **Inter-Relationship Marketing.**

Inter – because it is about how you interact with others

Relationship – because it is about getting and keeping contacts with others that work

Marketing – because it is a marketing based approach that treats others at work as customers not employees, and aims to get their 'buy-in'.

This is my passion. It's why I have written it for others like you to share.

Enjoy it!

Love it!

Hate it!

Just don't be indifferent. Be PASSIONATE!

Our emotions are what drive us and our organizations to incredible feats. Let them loose!

If you like *Passion At Work*, you may also enjoy the sister book to this for organizations, *Emotional Capital* (Capstone, 1998).

THE NEW DYNAMICS OF INTER-RELATIONSHIP MARKETING

Why use marketing in internal communication?

Marketing is a discipline and a philosophy that creates passion in its customers. Those who were passionate in the marketing profession developed now tried-and-tested strategies, processes, tools and techniques to keep their companies, brand, products and services one step ahead of the competition.

The marketing approach has some simple goals:

- find the 'hooks' that appeal to your target market
- persuade them to actually go out and buy the product or service
- keep them loyal and purchasing more – for life if possible.

Today we are all responsible for marketing ourselves and our ideas to everyone. Learning how to target your messages and finding the 'hooks' for each and every team member will be an important component of your marketing activity. And the key to it all is *communication*.

Interface or Internet?

CommunicationS versus communicatioN

Our knowledge of what makes the universe and the world around us tick – everything that is happening on the OUTSIDE of us – is increasing at a phenomenal rate. So too is our knowledge of what we know about everything INSIDE us. Yet while we are so advanced, and have now developed this super sophisticated world of communications and its new technological toys, it doesn't seem to have helped us with our communication with people.

Notice the difference in the last sentence between communication**S** – the **means** of delivery – and communicatio**N** – the ability to create common **understanding** between the giver and the receiver. This is vitally important in understanding which one is most useful to us.

When it comes to communication**S**, we all too often think if the message is sent then we have done our job. The proliferation of e-mail, company magazines and memos implies we have achieved massive communcatio**N** – but we haven't!

When it comes to communicatio**N**, it seems all too easy to upset people, often without realizing we have done it.

The challenge then goes beyond gaining understanding to gaining **buy-in**. It comes when we try to get people feeling positive about what we want them to hear. It is even more difficult when we know it's good for them to listen to what we have to say!

Getting buy-in goes beyond communication**S**, beyond communicatio**N** – it is here we move into marketing, which is what this book is all about.

Tick For Success

❏ Do you want to feel a passion for your work, that you know exists for some of the other great things in your life?

❏ Do you want other people as colleagues, team members or customers to understand and feel enthusiastic about what you want?

❏ Do you want people to see what you are trying to say and not get confused, annoyed, or angry?

❏ Do you want to hear the secret formula that will generate understanding and 'buy-in' as well?

❏ Do you want people to feel good about what you feel good about?

❏ Do you want to make your life easier by avoiding confusion and conflict with others at work?

❏ Do you want to understand why people sometimes say what they do and when they do?

❏ Do you want to get through to the opposite sex?

❏ Do you want to raise motivation and morale amongst people at work?

❏ Do you want to stop saying yes to these questions?

If you have ticked no to any of these, then perhaps you have misread the question! Of course you want to get a BIG YES to all of them.

How will this book help me?

This book covers two of the key parts of internal marketing. One of these is called research. You can call it 'getting to know people'. Without knowing your target audience then marketing is a pretty hit and miss affair. Once you have this in place you can go on to 'targeting'. This is how to create the right messages relevant to the researched market and using the right media – all of which gets buy-in to what you are saying.

The six *S*s

"
You are targeting your messages all the time. Here is a new way of honing your skills, and making life easier as a manager and leader.
"

Kathy Whitwell
co-developer
Passion At Work

Whether you are trying to understand and motivate an individual, a team, a department, a division, a company, a corporation or a global network you can only begin by understanding what each individual is like. Then and only then are you likely to find what will motivate them to buy-in to your messages. That is when you can target your message accordingly.

The Six *S*s will help you define what each individual is like. From there you can see how and where they fit into the overall picture of communication, with their team, boss, colleagues and the business.

Each of these Six *S*s is a subject in its own right. Together with the last section in this book they give you the HOW to creating passion at work. Here is a quick overview to let you see the big picture ...

SHAPES – your work style – the first S

"
This idea of using shapes to define my personality sounds decidedly unscientific, to put it mildly
"

Originally the concept of SHAPES was born from work with children. Researchers into child behavior noticed that children who were attracted to and continued to play with certain SHAPES of toys, acted and talked differently to those who liked to play with other SHAPES. It has even developed a name – geometric psychology.

More recently, communication consultants and occupational psychologists have used the SHAPES to astonishing effect to help people understand how they and others approach things in their lives. The great thing for you is that this knowledge can be used when you are formulating targeted messages for communication.

Using SHAPES that people relate to – like Squiggles, Boxes, Triangles and Circles – to assess their personality, really works. What's more, just think of the marketing implications when you are designing anything with graphics.

If Squiggles are people who don't like Boxes, then leave the Boxes out of your designs when targeting people with Squiggle tendencies!

And if Squiggles are people who speak a different language to Boxes, which they do, then watch out what you are saying to each of them. You will see what I mean when you read about SHAPES later in the book – it really is fascinating. As one person said on one of my workshops 'NOW I know why I keep clashing with my boss. It really has been harming my career. Just watch me get it right next time!'

Understanding SHAPES is the beginning of learning the dynamics of Inter-Relationship Marketing. The interplay that goes on under the surface of communication can be more than dynamic, it is often explosive.

The same applies to SHADES …

> "
> Yes, I'm a Triangle
> – that's why I want
> to see results –
> now!
> "

SHADES – your attitude – the second S

Our language is rich with expressions developed from the colors we associate with feelings. We use color to describe the attitudes and personalities of people around us – green with envy, red with rage, a shrinking violet, feeling blue, a black mood – our vocabulary reflects what we see.

A Swiss professor called Lüscher tested 60,000 people on the colors they liked and disliked, and rigorously researched what the choices signified. His findings have been used by people all over the world, both professionally in disciplines such as psychiatry, and – on a lighter note – simply for fun, whether at a party or in the pub. His book, the *Lüscher Colour Test*, has been hugely successful and is sold worldwide.

> "
> I've had my 'colors'
> done. I'm winter.
> Does this have
> anything to do with
> me coming across
> as cool?
> "

Others, such as Edward De Bono with his *Six Thinking Hats* and Gerry Rhodes and Sue Thane with *Colours of your Mind,* have used colour to describe phenomena such as idea creation and innovation.

Color consultancies also use color to show how to express the way we look and feel more effectively.

If you can't excite a Squiggle lover with a Box SHAPE then just think of the marketing implications of being so deeply attracted to colour that you can actually relate to it, and link it to your personality.

SEX – your gender – the third S

Gender psychology provides us with information on important differences, often big differences, between the sexes. It is another of our jigsaw pieces. It may sometimes seem like a pretty important piece, especially if you are a man trying to work in a group of women – and vice versa – so let's get 'sex' into perspective. Our gender still has a radical effect on the way we work.

The way whole organizations are communicating is moving from the male macho culture to a mixture of both male and female.

The old style approach of command and control arose out of a male dominant language and a male dominant society. Until recently men ruled the world of work, long before women even knew there was a glass ceiling. If you were a woman and you were always looking at the ground who cared if there was a ceiling! Now things are different.

The new style approach of self help and team working is just not the male way of doing things. Dare I say it is very much like the female style of communicating. A system of sharing and mutual appreciation as contrasted with instruction and leadership is much more a 'female' style.

SENSES – your experiences – the fourth S

The way we look at our own world and the senses we use most – sight, sound, touch – to get the best out of the information we give and receive affects our language and patterns of behavior.

The three key SENSES are described as: Visual (seeing) – Auditory (hearing) – Kinaesthetic (feeling). People who favor the different types of senses behave with different styles of speaking and acting.

Marketeers (my word for 'marketers' – I like to think of them as buccaneers), sales people, trainers and others whose role is to influence us know the power of using a range of different techniques to appeal to our senses.

Understanding the basic skills and techniques of getting buy-in by concentrating on what we see, hear, feel and think makes sense for everyone.

STATUS – your position in life – the fifth S

Our status at work is a reflection of where we 'sit' in the society we call work. Where we sit affects what marketeers call 'positioning'. Depending on your position you will change and adapt the positioning of your product, service or message to suit your target audience.

This positioning outside of work is heavily influenced by a number of factors including your childhood and your position in society. The position or status of your internal customer will likewise have an influence on what you say, how you say it and when you say it.

In some organizations fear of people's status and power higher up the organization leads to fear of communicating at all. But things are changing – rapidly!

SOCIAL – your money and your life – the sixth S

Your social influences, such as who you are (a Lord or a commoner, a Chief Executive or a street cleaner, a Brit or an Eskimo), where you live (high-rise apartment or stately home, condo or cabin), and your financial (how much you earn) factors ALL affect your life.

The financial and the social sides of your life will have an enormous influence on how you live and what you do and will affect you at work too. Marketing people have to take these into account the whole time. Think of the questions marketing people ask about you in the name of research …

Marketing research questions – getting to know you

- What do you buy?
- What are you thinking when you buy?
- When do you buy it?
- How do you feel about buying?
- How do you buy?
- How do you decide to buy?
- Who buys?
- Why do you change your mind?
- Where do you buy?
- Why do you stick to the same things?

More marketing research questions – really getting to know you

- What do you talk about?
- What do you say when you talk?
- How do you say it?
- Where do you say it?
- Who listens to you?
- Who influences you?
- What do you read?
- Who are your friends?
- How do you raise your children?
- Who are they talking to?
- What do they talk about? Etc.

All these questions – where do they lead?

It used to be that Lords and commoners, Chief Execs and street cleaners had a 'place' and they knew where it was. Now they have no place except as an equal member of society. They may have more or less money, influence and buying power, or they may think they have, but these days every vote counts, every pound or dollar spent counts and every individual counts – especially at work.

Who you are is no longer of as much importance in what is being seen as the true democratization of the world. In fact in business, downsizing and delayering has meant that there isn't that much status left!

Like attracts like and people of the same rank may club together outside work (whether for fun or security). At work, we now need to be able to communicate with everyone else, no matter what their STATUS – or SHAPE, SHADE, SEX or SOCIAL position.

Things ain't what they used to be. What they 'used to be' spawned a whole century's worth of management thinking. Is it all to be consigned to the dustbin of corporate history? Not while there are still those around who like to be more equal, or even superior. If 'I am the boss, and I like it that way' still applies to some people, then the old models need to be looked at. Why? Because these are the rules that your colleagues in this mode may be playing under.

The big picture – and the pieces

Every journey starts with one step – this one starts with SIX! Six steps that will lead you to some very exciting new places.

Do The T.W.I.S.T.T.

How will you get there? By doing the T.W.I.S.T.T.

Thomson **W**hitwell **I**ndicator of **S**tyle **T**ype and **T**argeting.

The T.W.I.S.T.T. is a brand new marketing tool that anyone can use. As its full name implies it is an indicator providing the basis of your research – getting to know your customer. It allows you to do two things:

- define people's **S**tyle – like how they like to work, e.g. organized or chaotic
- categorize their **T**ype – like are they outgoing or inward looking.

From there you can move into the second mode of marketing:

- **T**arget your message to capture their hearts and minds.

Let's T.W.I.S.T.T. again

As you begin to explore the Six *S*s of success both for yourself and with others, the windows onto the world inside their heads will open up for you. The T.W.I.S.T.T. is a fun, simple and easy way of helping you to do really understand 'where you are coming from'. You will learn how to understand better both yourself and others.

That's an overview of what we will be tackling in the next six sections. Now it's over to you. Let the **T.W.I.S.T.T. success generator** on the next two pages put it all together for you and give you a 'personal profile'. Try it out too on a colleague. The more you know, the easier it is to target your message.

As you go through the book, the answers revealing your choice of one symbol or another become clear. You can begin to build a picture that shows you why you answer the questions the way you do. Once you understand where you are coming from, then you can start to work on understanding your customers – be they internal or external. And the great thing is, once you know what makes them tick (and turns them on) ... creating passion at work is but a step away.

The T.W.I.S.T.T success generator

Part 1 – psychographics (your inner map)

T.W.I.S.T.T.

Circle what applies

What you say, do, think and feel:

Questions to ask yourself or others

Shapes

'Which shape do you prefer? Why?'
'What do you prefer: to create ideas and work on exciting new concepts or to apply tried and tested approaches? Why?'

'Which shape do you prefer? Why?'
'What do you base your decisions on: facts or feelings?'
'What is more important to you: efficiency and profit or support and buy-in from everyone involved? Why?'

Shades

'Which color do you prefer? Why?'
'Where do you draw your energy - from inside you or what goes on around you? Why?'

'Which color do you prefer? Why?'
'Do you prefer to leave everything to the last minute or plan your tasks way ahead? Why?'

Sex

'Describe a situation, where you worked really successfully with someone of the **same sex**. What was the secret of this success?'
'Describe a situation, where you worked with someone of the **same sex** and it didn't work out at all. Why did this happen?'
'Describe a situation, where you worked really successfully with someone of the **opposite sex**. What was the secret of this success?'
'Describe a situation, where you were working with someone of the **opposite sex** and it didn't work out at all. Why did this happen?'

Senses

'Tell me about your biggest success at work so far. Please try to recreate the scene in as much detail as possible for me. I'd like to be able to see what you saw, to hear what you heard and to understand how you felt.'

Status

'Remember a situation where you had to deal with a difficult client/ a challenging colleague. How did you deal with this situation? Describe in detail what you thought, did, said and felt.'

'How much responsibility do you have at work (e.g. how many people report to you)?'
'What do you like about having/not having responsibility?'

The T.W.I.S.T.T success generator

Part 2 – demographics (your outer map)

T.W.I.S.T.T.

Your influences

What you say, do, think and feel:

Questions to ask yourself or others

'Which country/countries had a significant influence on the way you think and act today? How would you describe this impact?'
'Where do you live now? How does this influence you?'

'What sort of community do you live in?'
'What's good about it?'
'What could be better?'

'When were you born?'
'How does your age affect your current feelings, actions and thoughts (e.g. did you think differently about a particular issue 10 years ago)?'

'What do you do for a living?'
'How does your job affect your beliefs and behavior?'

Social

'What income bracket do you put yourself in: Low, medium or high?'
'How does your income affect your lifestyle?'

'What religion or other beliefs do you have?'
'How does this affect your life?'

'What language(s)/dialects do you speak?'
'How does this affect the way you communicate with others?'

'What are the ethnic influences on you?'
'How do they affect your current lifestyle, feelings and actions?'

'Who are the key influencers from your family and friends?'
'How do they influence you?'

PART 2

THE SIX *Ss* OF SUCCESS AT WORK

Your Windows onto the Worlds of Other People, and Yourself

Know yourself and know others – it's a great start to success. Marketing people call it research.

Before you move on to targeting your message, it is a good idea to find out who it is you are targeting. Each of the six *S*s comes from a subject in its own right – get the hang of these and you will be amazed at what makes people tick and how you can use this knowledge to help you and them.

SHAPES:
THE FIRST S OF
SUCCESS

What SHAPE are you in, work-wise that is?

Do you know how your work style clashes or complements others?

Choosing the SHAPES will reveal a lot about you, and the people around you at work – so be prepared!

Understanding what people are like will help you to get what you BOTH want.

Shapes

What is this chapter about?

When it comes to getting buy-in to your messages your chances of success increase the more you target your messages to suit the person you're aiming at. The problem is you can't target your messages if you don't know what to look for.

SHAPES is the first of the six Ss to reveal a very important part of what to look for in your target market. SHAPES reveals people's work style. Are they creative, detailed, logical, feelings driven? Find out which of these types of personality people possess and you will begin to be able to recognize what they like, don't like and what will turn them on.

How you benefit – the hooks

SHAPES is the quickest, easiest, and most powerful way to discover someone's personality. You will become an instant wizard in psychology at work. The good thing for you is that it is more than a chapter on theory. At the end you will be given some practical skills showing you how to test and apply your marketing knowledge.

You will gain most by ...

... getting used to the ideas that personality determines how people like to receive information – not how you like to send it! Once you understand the reasons why people are different you will then begin to master communication and marketing skills by practising with the examples at the end of this chapter.

SHAPES – your work style

What makes you so different to those around you?

We have already established that people that like different SHAPES are different. We can add to this by dividing them into sets so that you can see the implications when we are defining work styles. Each of the two SHAPES in each set possesses different characteristics that make them opposite. The two SHAPES in each set are NOT JUST DIFFERENT – THEY ARE OPPOSITE.

You Choose

Remember to choose the symbol that best describes you. If you are stuck and don't know which one – ask yourself which one you most like or which one your eyes are drawn to.

These symbols represent your patterns of thought when it comes to how you organize and use information: they represent the INPUTS of your life and the way you use your thoughts, memories and emotions.

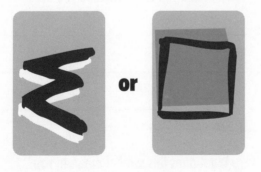

Squiggle or Box – who me?

Before moving on to our explanation of 'what you are like and why', take some time to think through your choice.

Why did you choose the one you did?

_____

_____

_____

What does this symbol mean to you?

_____

_____

_____

Why did you reject the one you did?

_____

_____

_____

What does this symbol mean to you?

_____

_____

_____

The Squiggle – what does it mean if I chose this one?

This is the symbol of the person who lives their life through ideas.

Squiggles love thinking for its own sake. They love creating new things out of the mass of information and ideas that spin around their heads.

Just look at the SHAPE. There isn't one thing going on, there are lots – Squiggles get off on variety. There isn't one direction the Squiggle is going in, there are lots of different ones – which reveals how they relish taking on a number of different challenges all at once. Yet at the same time, Squiggles seem to be going somewhere. It may look and be a chaotic symbol but it has a dynamic quality to it that says 'watch me and watch out'.

> *Ideas – don't you just love them?*

The Box – what does it mean if I chose this one?

This is the symbol of the person who lives their life through detail.

Boxes love information for its own sake. They get their information through using each of their senses to register facts, figures, faces, experiences. Boxes then organize this data in a way that allows them to put structure into this otherwise mad, mad world of ours.

> *Ideas people – they're so impractical.*

Look again at this SHAPE. It is solid, dependable and stable, all words that describe people who like to analyze problems and base their decisions on tangible evidence rather than intuition.

What is fascinating about these SHAPES, and all the other descriptions, is that almost everyone is proud of what they are – and have no idea how their opposite can live with the characteristic they are not!

Bo Derek was a 10 – are you?

Squiggles and Boxes – diametrically opposite

Did you choose the SHAPE that best describes you? If not, then change it. Just make sure that you are comfortable with the description. You have to be one or the other. While you may have some of the characteristics of each symbol in you, you can't be both a Box and a Squiggle.

Now try this test.

This is the advanced version of the choices you can make. You have 10 points to allocate to each of the symbols – AND YOU CAN'T SCORE 5 AND 5. How much of a Box or Squiggle are you?

	e.g.	Not	Your score
Squiggle	6	5	
Box	4	5	
Total	10	10	10
	✓	✗	✓

Whether you choose a Box or a Squiggle, your dominant symbol will determine the core characteristics of your work style. You will either organize your thoughts around facts and figures, or ideas.

What does this all mean?

You may be asking yourself what has this got to do with understanding people. To answer this question it is necessary to split the implications of people's choices into three headings. We call these the *three golden rules* of understanding types.

These are the three basic rules that emerge from being one or other of these symbols. These rules will apply to all the symbols in the T.W.I.S.T.T.

The three golden rules of understanding types

- **Golden rule 1 – process.** Your **process** of thinking is different. In other words the road you take with your thoughts is different depending on which symbol you choose.
- **Golden rule 2 – content.** Your **content** of thinking is different. In other words the drivers/motivators/inputs are different.
- **Golden rule 3 – language.** Your **language** is different. In other words the words/expressions/phrases you use to express your thoughts are different.

Remember process/content/language. Each symbol will expose a different part of you – or expose a different way with others.

The three golden rules applied to Squiggles

Golden rule 1 – their process of thinking

Squiggles like variety, particularly in conversation. They may take a scattergun approach to subjects and move quickly from one idea to another. Their speech tends to be fast and enthusiastic, demonstrating their sense of urgency and excitement. Their main course of action is to trust their instinct and believe in what they do and think. Why? Because they don't delve deep enough into the practical implications – they're simply turned on by ideas.

Golden rule 2 – the content Squiggles like

Here is a list of the things and that drive, motivate and inspire the Squiggle.

> *I think that is a brilliant idea, terrific. So are the other thirty-three. How soon can we try them ALL out?*

Ideas	Inspiration
Innovation	Change
Creativity	Future
Excitement	Abstract
Chaos	Possibilities
New	Different

These words describe what Squiggles like to think about – their content

Golden rule 3 – the language Squiggles like and use

Here is a list of clues for spotting a Squiggle in conversation.

> *I've been thinking. There are a number of different possibilities we could try out.*

'Great idea'
'What if ...'
'Here's what we could try ...'
'This could be interesting/different/new ...'
'Let's change the subject – this is boring ...'
'How about this ...'

So now we have it – process, content, language. We will use this approach throughout the book to describe what else makes people tick to help you understand them and their idiosyncratic ways.

Boxes – the symbol of thinking in detail

Golden rule 1 – the Box's process of thinking

Boxes aren't ones for social chitchat, preferring to stick to relevant facts and figures. They prefer an honest 'I don't know' to guesswork. Boxes feel more comfortable when the conversation is rational and realistic. They will always expect you to confirm everything in writing at the earliest opportunity.

Golden rule 2 – the content Boxes like

Here is a list of the things that describe and motivate Boxes.

Structured	Figures
Dependable	Schedule
Meticulous	Past
Factual	Dates
Reality	Task

This needs looking at in depth a lot more before we even think about what we might do.

Now if you are a Box you will like the look of these words. They may even bring a smile to your face! However if you are a Squiggle, even one mention of the word 'structured', let alone 'meticulous', will be enough to send you running!

Golden rule 3 – the language Boxes like and use

'Be specific'
'What are the facts and figures?'
'Can you be more accurate/objective?'
'Exactly what happened?'
'Precisely what did you do?'
'Logic demands ...'

It ain't what you say ...

You can now see that Squiggles and Boxes aren't just different ways of thinking, they are opposite.

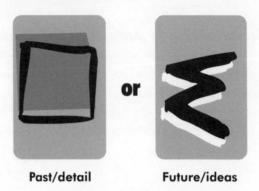

Past/detail   Future/ideas

Which are you? If you are a Squiggle guess what will happen when you come into contact with a Box? We're not just talking personality difference, but even personality clash. If we are, how will you deal with it?

Just think of the people you come into contact with. Are your colleagues in marketing a bunch of Squiggles? Are your colleagues in finance Boxes? Is it any wonder that Squiggles and Boxes don't see eye to eye, and may even upset each other? To illustrate, here is a typical Squiggle and Box conversation – You will no doubt recognize it, and perhaps have been part of it many times!

Squiggle
'I have a great idea. I want you all to stop what you're doing. This is the concept that will make us millions. It's great.'

Box
(Thinking) – Oh no, he's off on another crazy, hair-brained scheme. Can't he see we're all busy? Doesn't he realize we can't stop everything for his latest idea?

(Speaking) – 'We're a bit busy right now, can't it wait until later? We're in the middle of a detailed planning session.'

Squiggle
(Thinking) – What's up with them? They're always in a planning session, don't they ever DO anything – ideas are what drive a business. I'll go and find somebody else who might listen.

Box
(Thinking) – Oh good, he's gone; now we can get on with some *real* work.

Did you recognize the characteristics? And can you put some names of people you know to the SHAPES?

The differences between Squiggles and Boxes is not just a difference – it is a huge gulf. What's interesting is that the same gulf exists with the next two SHAPES, which define different characteristics.

Triangle and Circle

Look at the Triangle and Circle below.

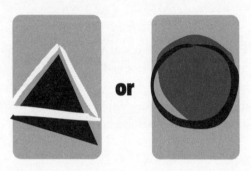

Remember, choose the symbol that best describes you (or pick the one you most like).

You can put your 'score out of 10' below.

Now, before moving on to our explanation of what you are like and why, take some time to think through your choice. Remember what we said earlier? – if you don't think it's you at first, then change your choice.

	Me	Someone you know
Triangle		
Circle		
Total	**10**	**10**

Remember – not 5 and 5! You are not allowed to sit on the fence.

Why did you choose the one you did?

_____

_____

_____

What does this symbol mean to you?

_____

_____

_____

Why did you reject the one you did?

_____

_____

_____

What does this symbol mean to you?

_____

_____

_____

Two ends of the 'ACTION' spectrum

Squiggles and Boxes are only half way to defining our characteristics, since they relate to our thought processes. However, we wouldn't get very far in life if all we did was think. Life is also about making decisions and acting on them. This is where Circles and Triangles come in.

The three golden rules of understanding types

Remember the 3 golden rules? These also apply to how you make decisions.

- **Golden rule 1 – process.** Your **process** for decisions is different.
- **Golden rule 2 – content.** Your **content** for making decisions is different.
- **Golden rule 3 – language.** Your **language** is different when talking about your decisions.

Triangles – the symbol of acting on facts

Golden rule 1 – the process for deciding

A Triangle's decision is based on weighing up the facts. People's feelings may be considered very carefully, however, it is likely that the head and not the heart will influence the final choice.

> *I have decided what you will all do.*

In simple terms Triangles make choices based on logic. They also find deciding very easy! This is because they are often very goal oriented. How to get what they want is very clear to Triangles.

Triangles prefer interactions that are direct, confident and to the point. Therefore it's wise to have a clear idea of what you want to say before starting a conversation with them. The sort of concepts they respond best to involve ways of helping them attain their goals or make more efficient use of their time. To Triangles, a brisk approach isn't unfriendly –it's desirable.

The main person in a Triangles life is 'I', in other words themselves. This means that their goals, hopes, ambitions and fears drive them to act. They act in a way that is decisive, telling others what to do and always with the end in sight. 'I know what I want, and I know how to get it' says a Triangle.

So whether it is bottom line profit, promotion to a job of higher grade, or a clear business result, Triangles will be very definite about what they want and what it will do for them. They want to improve their career and their bank balance.

If you just look at the SHAPES the Triangle is hard edged, angular, and pointed. In fact, it looks pretty much like the old corporate structure. For a Triangle there is only one place to be in the structure – you guessed it – at the top! They love to lead and not be led – they like to make the decisions not receive them.

Golden rule 2- the content Triangles like

Here is a list of the things that drive a Triangle to act:

Profit	Solutions (their own is best)
Goal	Brevity
Success (their own)	Truth (not politeness)
Control	Things versus people
Growth	Criticism (to make better)

Bottom line, top line – whose line is it anyway?

The quick-fire guide to an 'impersonal' Triangle is to remember:

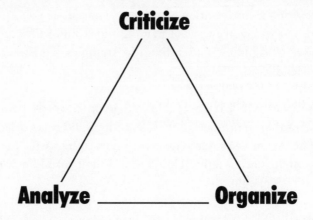

Golden rule 3 – the language Triangles like and use

'This has proved to work.'

'Have the results been established?'

'Let's get on with the job.'

'This plan has to be well thought through, including the people implications as well as the business goals.'

'Look what this can do for your career.'

'Never mind the waffle, just give me the bottom line.'

'That will work if you just (do as I say!) ...'

'Can you please cut the flannel and just give it too me straight.'

'Just give me the bottom line.'

'How much will this make?'

'What budget do you need?'

'I know I'm right about them/it/you no matter what anyone else says.'

The most important thing to recognize about Triangles is that they are not deliberately trying to upset you. Your feelings are just not as important as the facts. They will take them into account, but as part of an equation.

Circles – the symbol of acting on feelings

Golden rule 1 – the Circle's process for acting

Circles are 'people people'. They like people, they worry about other people, they take other people's feelings into account. Why? Because they love to know what others are doing, saying, thinking, feeling, believing.

> *You must be very concerned about the way things are going. If you need any help please give me a call.*

Circles may sometimes come across as more concerned for the well being of everyone else than themselves. And often they really are. However in their own way they are just as self centered as the Triangles. They love gossip for 'its own sake' and are often the type of person who loves talking about the latest incident in the office.

Circles are sociable people. They will begin a conversation by asking about your health, your family, even the weather – and will feel most comfortable if you do likewise. Circles appreciate someone who takes the time to listen to what they have to say in a warm, sympathetic manner. They may evenuse this as a clever ploy of their own, often getting you to say more about your true feelings than you originally planned to!

Golden rule 2 – the content Circles like

Here is a list of the content and concepts that turn Circles on – the language that makes their heads turn and listen:

People	Harmony (not conflict)
Feelings	Sentiment (not logic)
Team Work	Politeness (not truth)
Friendship	Agree (not disagree)
Chatting	Friendly (not business like)
Society	Charity (not selfishness)

Golden rule 3 – the language Circles like and use

'Are other people happy with this?'

'What do you think?'

'How does everyone feel about this?'

'Tell me again what he said.'

'I hope you feel good about this.'

'Let's go out for a bite and a chat.'

'Can we get together and talk it through?'

'I believe looking after staff is important.'

'What will the team think?'

'I feel so BAD about all these redundancies.'

'We can't possibly do that – people won't like it.'

'S/he didn't did s/he? Tell me more.'

The most important thing to remember about Circles is that they base their decisions on PERSONAL considerations, i.e. FEELINGS. They think more about how people will react and how people behave in certain situations than the 'facts of the matter'.

The old saying 'don't let your heart rule your head' is apt for describing Circles. When it comes to making decisions what they do, think and say is connected to their feelings. Thinking about one worried person may lead them to a course of action that a Triangle would consider and reject if the situation warranted it on facts alone.

While they are 'listening to you', they are fascinated and may find you interesting. But whether they agree with you is another matter.

SHAPES – a quick picture just to remind you

Squiggles – thinking creatively

Ideas going all over the place. Energy and enthusiasm sparking off everything they come into contact with.

Trusting their own intuition and belief in themselves and their ideas.

OR

Boxes – thinking in detail

Boxes build the fabric of society. Detail by detail, brick by brick they build solid structures.

Trusting to knowledge and information they write everything down in a detailed step-by-step process.

Triangles – acting on facts

Their goal is the most important thing of all. They lead and manage everything around them to reach their aim – and make sure they get to the top as a result.

OR

Circles – acting on feelings

People, people, people. The three most important things to Circles. Feelings are the key to their lives, their own, yours, everyone's. Add a smile and ears to the Circle to reveal their strengths. They are both friendly and great listeners.

Now it's your turn
The mental aerobics sections

The exercises at the end of each of the six Ss (in a box with a pencil icon like this) are designed to achieve three main objectives:

- get you to think like the other person
- show you how to use the right words to ensure they want to listen to you
- give you practice with situations where you need to use your knowledge of them to help you both achieve what you want.

And one other objective:

- to have fun!

Mental aerobic exercise no. 1:
SWOT a Box
(and a Squiggle, Triangle and Circle)

The best way to really understand someone is to ask them what they are like! When you talk to them the trick is to write down their exact words as they speak. Their quotes will point the way to understanding how to approach them from now on.

This exercise takes the classic marketing tool of SWOT, using Strengths, Weaknesses, Opportunities and Threats to get your target customer talking about themselves. This is a subject most people love to talk about! It will provide you with a mine of information.

Name _____

Their SHAPES   Squiggle or Box _____
                      Triangle or Circle _____

Strengths
'What is good about being you?'
e.g. to a Squiggle – 'Do you love coming up with new ideas. Why do you?'

Weaknesses
'What could be better about being you?'
e.g. to a Box – ' Do you find it difficult understanding creative people?'

Opportunities
'What new things do you see for you in the future?'
e.g. to a Triangle – 'Where do you see your career taking you?'

Threats
' What could stop you achieving what you want?'
e.g. to a Circle – 'Do you worry too much about what other people think?'

Mental aerobic exercise no. 2: Persuade the boss – a Triangle

Your boss is a Triangle. You are a Squiggle and have a great new idea. In the past your boss seemed to listen to your ideas, and was enthusiastic at the time but nothing much seemed to happen after that.

Now is your chance to use Triangle language to put your case differently. You can use benefits that your boss will see as benefits, not that you think are benefits. Prepare your case using the format below.

The structure below is one we will use later and you have already come across it as chapter headings. It is based on a formula called WHY Communicate™. The format has been tried and tested on thousands of managers and staff – of all SHAPES. Fill out the answers first. Practice it as a script on any Triangle. See which parts work and why. Once you have the structure of WHY Communicate and you know what your target customer is like, you are well on the way to becoming a persuasive communicator and maybe even a great marketeer.

*W*hat is this about?

Describe in Triangle language what you want to talk about, e.g. 'Chris, I have a powerful concept for you to consider to improve productivity and the quality of our products.'

*H*ow you benefit

Describe in Triangle terms the benefits to the Triangle and to the organization of adopting your idea, e.g. 'The great thing for you is that this idea will make you, and all of us in our department, look like we are delivering better returns by being proactive.'

*Y*ou will gain most by ...

... showing what YOU want to happen now that you have your Triangle hooked, e.g. 'What I would like to do is to pull together a task team, with your support and leadership to see how we might pilot this idea, and asses the bottom line business benefits.'

Mental aerobic exercise no. 3:
Getting a different perspective

You want help. You have a problem or challenge, or you need to be creative, and you don't know what to do. You need a different perspective from another SHAPE.

Seeing things from someone else's point of view is good – for you and them. What is even better is if they are a different SHAPE to you. Try it and see.

My challenge is _____

I need help on _____

The Squiggle's ideas:

The Box's considered opinion:

The Triangle's logical point of view:

The Circle's feelings on the matter:

Mental aerobic exercise no. 4: Write an internal 'advert'

You want to attract a certain type of person – it may be an event you want to run. You need to write an advert. It can go out in any format you chose, from an e-mail to a Web page to a poster on the notice boards. Here are some titles (in bold) you might like to attempt to attract each of the SHAPES – or think up your own!

- Attract the Squiggles – **Brainstormers wanted**
- Attract the Circles – **Help required for social events**
- Attract the Triangles – **Dynamic project leaders required**
- Attract the Boxes – **Workers on a task force needed.**

Studies also show that in large groups ALL of the SHAPES are fairly evenly distributed. How would you attract everyone?

- **Open day for local community – help of all types needed.**

Your advert

SHADES – THE SECOND
S OF SUCCESS

How colorful is your language?
What SHADES of expression do you use?

How much does people's attitude to work help or hinder?

Which color people choose reveals a lot about them and their approach to life.

SHADES allows you to determine some of the key motivators and how best to get through to people.

Shades

What is this chapter about?

Through the last chapter on SHAPES, you now know about people's style at work and how it affects the way they like to receive messages and act on them. Great, and there is more! The way people approach life is as important as the way they approach a task. Are they outgoing, inward looking, do they like things organized or do they like things left flexible? In this chapter, SHADES will give you an understanding of the way people like to interact with others, and how they see the world around them.

How you benefit

The most powerful aspect of SHADES is that it will help you get straight to the heart of the person you are looking to get on your side. With this information you will be able to create tremendous rapport. You will be able to develop a respect for people's approaches, because you'll 'know where they are coming from'. You will feel better about them. They will feel better about you.

You will gain most by ...

... thinking about the people you know as you read the chapter. You can begin to try out on them some of the language they like, to check if it works! At the end of this chapter are more practical ideas to explore the ways to get to understand people, get buy-in to your messages, and deliver better business results.

Shades – your attitude

What makes you so different to those around you?

SHADES are another way of learning about yourself and the people around you. Some people call it color psychology – we've called it SHADES. The techniques are very similar, using color as a means to describe personality.

Just like the SHAPES, there are two sets of SHADES. Each of the two SHADES not only possesses different characteristics, but once again the two colors in each set are also opposites.

What this means for you is that if you are one SHADE in a set, you may find it very difficult to understand, get to know, or communicate with your opposite. They say opposites attract. They may well do. They can be very complementary. Opposites can also wind each other up into coiled springs ready to go ping at any time. Here is the first set:

YOU CHOOSE – What sort of person am I?

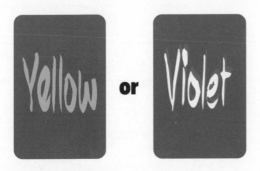

Remember, choose the SHADE that best describes you. If you are stuck choose the one that you like most.

You know the rules by now and remember sometimes people choose the SHADE for 'untypical' reasons. If so, you can change your choice by knowing why you chose this SHADE in the first place.

Why did you choose the one you did?

_____

_____

_____

What does this symbol mean to you?

_____

_____

_____

Why did you reject the one you did?

_____

_____

_____

What does this symbol mean to you?

_____

_____

_____

Yellow or Violet – the inside and outside of your focus on the world

These colors represent how you live in your world and describe your attitude to dealing with your environment.

They are best represented by the classic terms of introversion and extroversion. Often we use these to describe loud people – extroverts, and quiet people – introverts. This is an example of language which has become somewhat misused.

> *The only way to get noticed in this organization is to STAND OUT.*

The original terms for 'extroversion' or 'introversion', invented by Carl Jung, relate to where people get their energy – from what goes on outside them, or their own internal thoughts and feelings. Extroverts are people who are more involved with what is going on OUTSIDE them. Introverts are people who are more involved with what is INSIDE them.

The real test of whether someone is introverted is to put them alone on a deserted mountain where they will be in their element. Put an extrovert alone and after a short time he or she will start heading for the nearest village, just to have someone to talk to!

> *I wish they'd all go away so I can concentrate.*

These behavioral patterns are the fundamentals of choosing the SHADES Yellow or Violet. Violet signifies introversion, Yellow extroversion.

The three golden rules applied to Yellow and Violet

Remember:

- golden rule 1 – process
- golden rule 2 – content
- golden rule 3 – language.

Yellow – the color of extroversion

Golden rule 1 – the process of living

Yellow is the color of a person who draws their energy and vitality from what happens outside them – the extrovert. They often see Yellow as the rays of the sun and link it to motivation and excitement. The bright color of Yellow gives them a feeling of vibrancy, elation and enthusiasm.

Yellow people are more externally focused and like to investigate things in a broad-ranging way so that they can apply this experience and knowledge to the many and varied experiences they seek. They like to act quickly and spontaneously. Just like the sun coming up with its rays touching the world, so the Yellow person will want to communicate. Being broad ranging they will express their thoughts, ideas, actions or feelings not only on a one to one basis, but to spread their influence to as many as possible.

Golden rule 2 – the content Yellows like

Here is a list of personality traits and characteristics that depicts how a Yellow person lives life:

- talks without thinking
- thinks with their mouth open
- lives life now – impulsive
- loves experiencing what is happening
- tries it out expecting it to work out
- acts first thinks later
- experiences emotions easily and often
- flits across the surface of lots of issues
- often outspoken – can put their foot in it
- feels down if left alone.

Golden rule 3 – the language Yellows like and use

'Let's have some fun'
'Here's something exciting'
'Can do'
'Do it now'
'Great opportunity – go for it'
'I'm surprised that worked/didn't work!'

The most important thing to remember about Yellow people is that they suck their energy from everything around them. They invariably like emphasis on 'action packed' concepts. Liking action, they move and think quickly. They are therefore not very good with long, complicated work or ideas.

Yellow people are often good at expressing their own point of view and communicating their thoughts to other people. They don't mind being interrupted and will even go out of their way to interrupt other people if they need some contact themselves. They want lots of praise. They like to have people tell them how good they are – not just occasionally but all the time.

The good news is that Yellows are in the majority. According to research by Myers Briggs, nearly three-quarters of all people are extrovert. This is particularly advantageous if you are an outward-facing person as you'll instantly know how to relate to most people.

Violet – the color of introversion

Golden rule 1 – the Violet process of living

Violet people draw their energy and strength from what happens inside them. Their way of living is inside their minds, not outside. The phrase 'shrinking violet' rather unfairly depicts a person who is introverted. The quiet ones – male or female – may say little and keep a low profile but the chances are they're thinking – and pretty in-depth thoughts too.

Just because they are not talking doesn't mean there is nothing happening in their heads. The problem for Violets, especially when they become members of a team, is that they are seen as less able or unwilling to contribute. Their Yellow colleagues may be much faster, but a Violet will study, analyze and think through the results of their actions. Where a Yellow might say 'Great! – let's do it' a Violet will usually sit and ponder on it before even opening their mouth. A Yellow experiences life, warts and all. This is their main reason for living – that's why they rush into situations to experience them sooner! The Violet will think things through in a considered way. This can best be summed up as:

> *I find it difficult to express myself. I feel like I am exposing my soul.*

'Yellows go wide, Violets go deep.'

Golden rule 2 – the content a Violet likes

Here are the personality traits and characteristics that typify the Violet approach to life:

- may like people but needs time alone
- enjoys sustained focus on one subject
- likes working alone
- thinks without talking

- thinks before speaking, may act too late
- prefers small numbers – good at one to one
- may be slow to make friends, but keeps them
- holds back energy
- keeps real self hidden
- lets others talk first
- likes peace and quiet to concentrate
- avoids bold, sweeping statements
- very interested in what goes on behind things.

Violets are like still waters – they run deep. Dealing with Violets can be difficult for Yellows, so here are two tips for successful relationships:

- **Tip 1 – when they speak – listen.** They are making an effort to express themselves and it will be worth listening carefully.
- **Tip 2 – when they don't speak ask them to talk – it will be worth getting their opinion.** Hearing Yellow people express their news and views all the time can be very one-sided and lacking in deep thought and reasoning.

What I need is some peace and quiet. Then I will get some real work done, without all this constant interference.

Golden rule 3 – the language Violets like and use

Violet people are mostly quiet so it's not hard to spot them! You might hear these kinds of expressions at work:

'I need time to think more deeply'
'I enjoyed working alone on this long term project'
'Why are we doing this? (look for lots of questions)
'I haven't thought this through carefully enough'
'Perhaps'
'Maybe if ...'
'Let's not jump to conclusions'.

The most important thing to remember about Violet people is that they get their energy from INSIDE and are more focused on intangibles like ideals and concepts.

Some people are Red, some people are Blue
Say the wrong words and it backfires on you

Red or Blue? – you choose

Choose the SHADE that best describes you:

Now you've got one more set of opposite SHADES to choose from!

These SHADES represent how you deal with what is going on in the world. Yellow and Violet dealt with your attitude to the world. Red and blue deals with HOW you put things into practice – whether you like to think before you make decisions, or whether you like events to happen before the deciding part has to take place.

Why did you choose the one you did?

_____

_____

_____

What does this symbol mean to you?

_____

_____

_____

Why did you reject the one you did?

_____

_____

_____

What does this symbol mean to you?

_____

_____

_____

What do they reveal about you?

Do you see life as a series of decisions to make before the event, or do you see life as a series of events to watch and weigh up leaving the decisions until the last minute? These questions are answered by your choice of red or blue.

Red – the color of emotion

Golden rule 1 – the Red process is 'think as you go, decide only when you must'

> *Oh, I will do that on Thursday. It isn't needed until then.*

Red is the color of warmth, emotion and, of course, anger. It is the color of the character best described as 'playful'.

The Red person likes to think about the situation and make it up as they go along, even if they don't carry it out in the end. So Red relates to the Squiggle or Box parts of the T.W.I.S.T.T. Blue relates to the Triangle or Circle. If you choose red you choose the 'thinking' mode over decisions, and your most preferred SHAPE has to be either a Squiggle or Box. If you are a Squiggle you will be making up lots of ideas and creating lots of possibilities about what might be done. If you are a Box you will be sorting out the detail from past experience in order to decide what might be done this time.

The key word to a Red person is MIGHT. They might do one thing, they might do another. They will probably NEVER have all the information they need, so making a decision is really hard.

Golden rule 2 – the content Reds like

- flexibility
- change
- new jobs, opportunities
- leaving decisions to the last minute
- things that are open ended
- different ways of looking at things
- nonconformity
- the unexpected.

I love leaving things until the last minute – it's so exciting!

Red people prefer to play rather than plan. If they are a Box they prefer to play with detail. If they are a Squiggle they play with ideas. They enjoy doing lots of thinking about lots of things. They know there is a world of information, knowledge, choice and perceptions out there and they love hearing about it. They happily stay in this world before having to decide what to do with all this information they have.

Because they need all the knowledge they can, they often only act at the last minute – just in case they might have missed something.

Why do it today if you can put it off till it needs to be done?

Golden rule 3 – the language Reds like and use

'Leave that work till later – let's do this first, it's more fun'
'I'm sure it will sort itself out'
'I'll arrange that when the time comes'
'It will be all right on the night'
'I'm working on lots of things right now'
'Let's go with the flow'
'Don't pin me down'
'Don't worry, there's lots of time'
'Stop organizing me, I'm fine'.

Most of all, Reds like things to be open-ended. Life to them is an open book with plenty more pages to turn, read, write and find out about. They like to gather as much information as they can before deciding what to do with it. To a Red this is not being indecisive. It is being sensible. 'Why decide', they argue, 'when you haven't got all the information/details/ideas that you need?'

Reds keep their minds open and like to leave their diary or calendar unbooked. Who knows what better opportunity may present itself, even at the last minute?

In summary they play, not plan, they like to take risks, always doing things at the last minute which to others seems crazy, yet to them it makes sense. Leaving things closed means there's no opportunity to change which a Red hates. Talking of closed, hot blooded Red has its opposite in cool Blue.

Blue – the cool color

Golden rule 1 – the Blue process is planning ahead

Where is my diary organizer? I need to update my action list.

Blue is the color of cool clear water. Unlike Red with its emotional overtones, a person who is Blue likes the feeling of calmness and peacefulness. Blue is the color of cool, clear and logical thinking, not for its own sake but in order to take action.

It is the color of the person who makes decisions before they act. They will jump in, dive in, ease themselves in or not go in at all but they will take the plunge sooner rather than later. If they (or you) are a Triangle, decisions will be based on impersonal facts, figures and measured outcomes. They will take others' feelings into account, but are more driven by the need to progress. Nothing and no-one will get in the way of the decision.

Circles base their decisions and judgement on their feelings about other people. They will, however, make a judgement. If they like you – great. You are part of their 'in-crowd'. If you cross them – beware. They can bear a grudge forever. You are GUILTY or NOT GUILTY – and this will stay with them. There is no middle ground.

Blue people are always able to make a decision about something. Some will decide even if there is not enough information, others will choose to wait. They don't leave things to the last minute. They are not hot-headed. They wait for the right moment calmly and peacefully – unless someone or something gets in the way. Then they can go into Red – in a big way!

Golden rule 2 – the content Blues like

diaries	oustoms	
deadlines	habits	
decisions	conforming	
organization	definite choices	
structures	the expected	
urgency	actions	
getting things done	promptness	
being purposeful	telling	
standards	being right!	

> *I have decided what needs doing and when. I also have a good idea who will do what, and how I would advise them to do it.*

Red people prefer to play. Blue people prefer to plan. Of course Blues will have some fun, as long as they have planned it first.

Golden rule 3 – the language Blues like and use

'Let's plan this first'

'We need to get this sorted and out of the way before we move on'

'I don't care if it's wrong, I have decided'

'I'm not interested in adding more to my list, there is enough to do already'

'I've got enough to go on – let's stop all this background stuff'

'How long will it take you?'

'What do you mean you don't know when we will arrive. I have to know!'

'The room is booked, the schedule is completed to the last detail, your flight is organized. Everyone did everything I asked them to do. It will run like clockwork.'

Blues most of all like things that are CLOSED – decisions that have been made, and bridges that have been crossed. Life to them is like sitting in a court behaving as judge or jury – they weigh up the facts and decide what to do, say or think. Once they have convicted, they plan what should happen and for how long. Guilty or innocent? A Blue will decide, whereas a Red will never really know, if they feel they don't have all the facts.

Summary – SHAPES and SHADES:
your work style and attitude to life

SHAPES and SHADES provide the core characteristics that make up the basis of your personality – the central structure to your complicated self. Once you know what these characteristics are, you can determine how you and other people are likely to react in most situations.

While life obviously isn't as easy as four SHAPES and four SHADES, this is a great start to recognizing what people are like. If SHAPES and SHADES interest you then I recommend that you investigate Myers Briggs, where you will recognize the similarities between their descriptions of type and those of Geometric and Color Psychology. You will also recognize the descriptions in SHAPES and SHADES in many other tests, such as Belbin, which uses descriptions like 'Plant', rather than a Squiggle.

It is at this point of describing 'type' that the psychometric tests stop short. There are many other factors beyond those covered in psychological tests that add further characteristics to our make up. These factors also contribute to what and who we are. For example, a female Squiggle is quite different to a male Squiggle, as you will discover in the next chapter.

Shapes and Shades of personality
– and more to come

Mental aerobic exercise no. 5:
What makes you tick?

'I want to be able to work better with you. We somehow seem to rub each other up the wrong way. I don't intend it to happen, and I am sure you don't, to but it just happens. I know we are not getting the best out of each other.'

You may be saying something like this with someone at work – the problem is you just don't know how to tackle it.

Why not try the SHADES approach below to get to understand them better. Are they Yellow or Violet? Are they Red or Blue? Whichever of the two sets of colors they are you will be able to ask them some searching questions like those below in a non-threatening way using the colors as the basis for your discussion.

What I like is ...

Yellow questions
How do you best like to work – with others or alone? (You know the answer to this, if they have chosen the 'right' color.)

_____

_____

What do you most like to talk with others about? (You will find out their interests, and therefore their 'hooks'.)

_____

_____

Violet questions

How do you best like to work – with others or alone? (You also know the answer to this, if they have chosen the 'right' color.)

_____

_____

When it comes to work, what do you spend most time thinking about?

_____

_____

Red questions

Which do you prefer, to be organized, or to leave things more flexible? Why? (You know the answer to this, if they have chosen the 'right' color.)

_____

_____

How would we work best together; should we agree to play it by ear?

_____

_____

Blue questions

Which do you prefer, to be organized, or to leave things more flexible? Why? (You also know the answer to this, if they have chosen the 'right' color.)

_____

_____

SEX – THE THIRD S OF SUCCESS

Are organizations changing sex?

How will learning about the differences between men and women help me?

Why do men, on average, spend 3 minutes on the phone and women spend 23?

What can men and women learn from each other about the way they communicate?

This chapter explores these gender issues and lets you draw your own conclusions.

Sex

What is this chapter about?

This chapter is about the differences between the genders. Differences that are not better or worse, just differences. Gender at work is clearly a 'hot potato', and a fundamental part of the marketing mix in understanding internal and external customers.

How you benefit – the hooks

This chapter lays down some very simple rules about understanding gender differences. These simple rules will show you how to adapt your behavior in today's masculine and feminine driven organizations.

You will gain most by ...

... trying to see things through the eyes of the opposite sex so you can begin to suspend judgement about the rights and wrongs of their approach.

Sex

Does your gender really make a difference? If it does – how great is the difference between male and female?

To demonstrate that it may be more than just a difference, here is a piece of real dialogue between three people – two females and one male. To start with, the conversation has one key ingredient exposed – their main SHAPE, and one key ingredient hidden – their gender. Try and see if you can spot the difference between 'his' and 'hers'.

The Scene – in the corridor at work

Triangle talks to Box and Squiggle

 'Oh, by the way, can we get together in 10 minutes to talk about D?' (D is a business contact) 'We need to agree where we are going with him.'

 'Yes, that sounds good to me. There are a number of important points that need to be worked out.'

 'Great.'

At the meeting:

 'I'll kick off. From what I can see we seem to be putting a lot into our relationship with D and not getting as much out.'

 'OK, what are we going to do about it?'

'Each time we give more information away D seems to take it and not give us much credit.'

 'Right. What do you suggest we do?'

 ' Recently he even quoted "ABC", our competitor, at a talk he was giving. He quoted them without even mentioning our work with him at all. Can you believe that!'

 [*Getting annoyed*] 'I get the message! What do you want me to do? I have been throwing him lots of ideas, to try to get him involved. I'm sure it will work out.'

 'And do you know what really makes me angry? All that detailed work we conducted for our joint project is not being mentioned at all in another talk he is giving on the subject at a conference.'

 'Look, you seem to be suggesting I have made a bad choice here.'

 'No, it's not your choice. What makes me so cross is that D seems to be taking advantage of us.'

 [*Getting angry*] 'Right. You are saying all the time I've spent with D is totally wasted. I'll look for someone else to work with, but I don't see who we can go with. I know you have been busy but I don't see you two helping me on this. In fact the work you were supposed to help me do didn't get done.

 [*Trying to conciliate*] 'We are not suggesting anything drastic yet. We are just looking for a way to work effectively together for the future'.

[Getting angry as well] 'I simply wanted to show how each time we try working together we lose out. You are now suggesting I have failed to complete my work. Everybody seems to be blaming everyone else and I'm not having it. I'm going.'

 [Speaking to box] 'Don't go.' (Leaves to console Box)

 'I can't understand this. You are telling me I've really messed up and you are the ones now getting upset and leaving!'

Did you spot the genders? Go back and read the conversation again with a new insight:

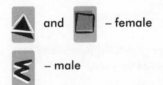

The reason this conversation ended in conflict, anger and created a potential rift between the people involved, was that the differences between the genders created a divide which neither side could understand or cross. This conversation as you will see later illustrates that gender makes a **very big difference** to the way people are, and that the **divide can be enormous** between male and female.

Sex – a three-letter divide

Once you begin to understand the opposite sex and start to build a bridge, then you can begin to minimize the differences and help yourself to cross to the other side.

The following grid provides an overview – a top of the jigsaw box – of the key words and symbols in our three letter memory jogger.

SEX – a three-letter mnemonic

Female

 = **Share**

Women like to talk, listen, discuss issues and get other people involved.

They come up with the answers through sharing their thoughts and emotions. Sharing can take time and is considered important.

 = **Enhance/Exaggerate**

Women like to emphasize what has happened and how they feel.

Exaggeration adds power to the conversation, expressing feelings that are being made abundantly clear, and often only to other women.

 = **Push/Pull**

This is the symbol of moving towards or moving away – with few overtones of superiority.

Women see others as equals whom they push away or pull towards them.

T H E   G R E A T   D I V I D E

Male

 = **Solve**

Men like to provide solutions, give answers, show they know what to do.

Unless they have specifically asked for it, they usually don't want advice and prefer short, sharp conversations that get right to the point. Sharing is not important, solutions are.

 = **Explain**

Men give facts, figures and feelings as they are, with little or no exaggeration.

They also expect facts, figures and feelings given them to be as correct and precise.

 = **Order/Obey**

This is the symbol of command and control – with overtones of superiority.

Men see communication in terms of order and obey or the role of the subordinate and subservient.

Commanding, and ordering or obeying, is the natural male orientation. If you know more than me, they think, I'll defer to you and vice versa.

Sex and the structure of society and organizations

There have been many theories behind the origins of gender difference and most recently Deborah Tannen and John Gray have made the subject even more talked about.

These theories point to one pretty obvious conclusion.

> I like yes men – they always do as I say.

Men and women are different!

The hierarchical nature of organizations has reflected the male way of behaving for centuries; from ancient military organizations like Genghis Khan or the Roman Army (male and triangles) to administrative organizations like the original Chinese bureaucratic order (male and boxes). More recently these male structures have survived, grown and been carefully nurtured in industrial organizations – by men (patriarchal and autocratic). See *Emotional Capital*, the sister/brother to this book, for more on this.

From the industrial revolution to post-war companies, order and obey, or command and control, was the (male) order of the day.

> These men, they are always exaggerating everything, especially about how important they are.

In primitive society females didn't adopt the same way of working as males because the nature of their work did not demand it. Their role was to encourage communication with their children, to foster a learning environment and to promote the same within the tribe as a whole. This nurturing and team working role is among the strengths of organizations today.

For females, the male role of order and obey, and dealing in facts is unnecessary. Females see others predominantly as equals. There is no need for a hierarchical structure when females get together. People are either part of their specific 'in crowd' of acquaintances and friends, or they aren't. So instead of order and obey the mode becomes one of 'push or pull'. Either we're friends, or we're not.

> She is such a good boss; she listens a lot. I just don't like the fact she got my job.

More recently, modern psychological work with children has also pointed to the differences in the way girls bond with other girls in this 'push-pull' manner. Little boys form gangs with clear leaders and hierarchies, in an order–obey mode, whereas girls form groups of friends based on the 'in-crowd' concept and 'best friends' which seem to fluctuate according to which girl is being pulled towards or pushed away from the other.

In a world where men and women now live and work together, these **opposite** characteristics of Male and Female are the ones which cause friction, misunderstanding and ultimately relationship breakdowns.

Until recently society had been organized around the separate characteristics of the two genders. Women and men did their own thing. NOW they are working TOGETHER.

Organizations are changing sex!

With a move from order and obey to empowerment, people can only persuade others. This requires everyone to use a push and pull type communication. Which gender model is this?

Life at work is now much too complicated for people to attempt to be better or think they are better than all those others who are now specialists at their job. Now people are having to 'ask' and 'listen' not 'tell' and 'sell'. Which gender model is this?

On top of the structural changes to organizations something else has happened. More women are now in work and are becoming increasingly important in the work they do. Part-time working favors some women because of their combined domestic role. Team working also favors women because of the way they work together in a collaborative fashion. Structurally, as well as in the ways of working, organizations are changing towards female role models.

However, men still account for the majority of senior positions in major organizations – although the overall mix in all organizations is levelling out.

If organizations are to get the best of both worlds they need to become both Female AND Male.

This means two languages, two structures and two different ways of working. NOT ONE – TWO. This is a huge and fundamental paradigm shift. Are YOU ready, never mind your organization?

The big question is ...

... **are organizations ready for this sex change?**

The problem is that no-one has taught today's males and females that they are now living in a different world.

Equal and opposite – a recipe for disaster?

The conversation between colleagues (the Squiggle, Triangle and Box) at the beginning of this chapter highlighted the conflict in behavior that can occur between different genders. This clash of gender was in addition to the friction between the three types of personalities. The Triangle wanted things sorted; the Box wanted the detail analyzed; the Squiggle wanted to get on with anything at all and not be tied down to a plan or details. On top of all of this the gender divide got in the way.

In the past it would have been easier. The male (boss) would have 'won'. He would have 'ordered' the employee (female) to do whatever he saw fit, with not much, if any, question of gaining agreement or consultation. Now everyone is equal – and expected to communicate effectively without any real hierarchy imposing its iron will.

An exchange of views is now beginning to be recognized as necessary by everyone. Today's buzz word is 'buy-in'. This needs to be obtained from everyone so that you all agree a course of action together.

But when we try to do that we have a problem.

Men and women are talking a different language and operating in a different way!

This fundamental difference is what creates the Great Divide between the sexes.

The way forward is now empowered teams, people delivering results through co-operation.

A.N. Optimist

The Great Divide – two languages, two structures

Unfortunately many men and women aren't aware how wide this divide is. To make the situation even more complicated, men are still operating in a 'top down' organizational mode.

We all understand that the percentage of women who are now at work is much higher. But are people communicating any differently?

Susan, it's so good to hear from you. You will never guess what we are doing these days in our division ...

Women are better at 'listening with' people, discussing what has happened and trying to reach consensus as to what to do about it. Research by BT illustrates that because men feel no need to 'share' the time they spend on the phone is minimal. The reverse is true for women.

On average, men spend only 3–5 minutes on personal telephone calls, whereas women spend 20–25 minutes in conversation. It is not uncommon to hear a man saying 'Why doesn't she hurry up and get on with it?' It is also not uncommon to hear a woman say 'You are so abrupt.'

To understand the differences in communication between men and women we are not only concerned with how long they speak, i.e. **the number of words**, but also **what is said** and **how it is said**.

In analyzing how well we are doing with the opposite sex we need to concentrate on all three.

The chart 'The Great Divide' provides a simple visual diagram of all the differences between the sexes in communication. As you will see, they are on opposite ends of the spectrum.

The Great Divide – two languages, two structures

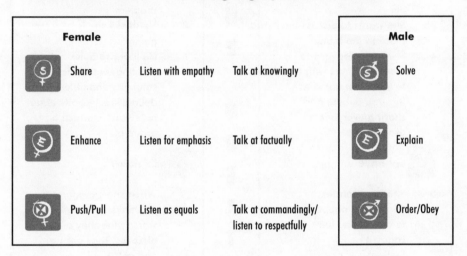

The best description of the difference can be summed up in this wonderful two-liner:

Men try to be interesting

Women try to be interested

Top ten conflicts in the Great Divide at work

Female

 Share

1. She wants to talk it over
2. She wants a sympathetic ear
3. She wants to discuss her place in the team
4. She looks forward to team meetings with time to tease out answers through debate and sharing everyone's experiences.

 Enhance

5. She exaggerates things that happen to emphasize her concern or feelings
6. She discusses her feelings with emphasis
7. She clearly shows she is upset.

 Push/Pull

8. She will help out others and give advice where she thinks it is needed
9. The more she likes him the more she helps (pulls by giving advice)
10. The more she communicates with him the worse it gets and she doesn't know why.

THE GREAT DIVIDE

Male

 Solve

1. He wants her to stop talking
2. He wants to solve her problem
3. He thinks she is gossiping
4. He looks to quick meetings with quick solutions and little debate – especially about his solutions which he is proud of.

 Explain

5. When she exaggerates he thinks things are worse than they are – discovers they are not and gets mad
6. He may not want to hear about feelings, certainly not strong ones.
7. He thinks he must hold back and complains of 'emotional women'.

 Order/Obey

8. He sees her advice as standing on his toes
9. Other men see her advice to him as him losing status
10. The more she gives advice the more he thinks that she is saying he is incapable.

The bottom line

Organizations are running at only 50–60% efficiency in communication. The gender differences play a big part in this. This adversely affects the top line and the bottom line and ultimately, in this highly competitive world, the future of every organization.

Sex – the answer sealed with a KISS

What do you do about the differences in order to build a bridge over the Great Divide? There are three things you can use for each of the three letters in the SEX mnemonic to help your communication.

The same approach to dealing with differences between people is also used to deal with the differences as in SHAPES, SHADES and all the Ss.

It's time to move into How Tos!

Here they are:

1   **Celebrate the differences.** Welcome the different views you are getting from all these different people because they are what they are, not what you want them to be. Recognizing, and even celebrating the differences will help make it less painful for you when dealing with them and much more interesting.
2   **Watch, match and nudge.** This is the crux of the *How Tos*. First **watch** people, then **match** your language and behavior to theirs. Only then do you **nudge** them forward. This means that you tune into your recipient's wavelength, match your language to theirs to make them feel like you are close to their way of thinking; then you can start to influence them gently and begin to move them forward (this method is explained later).

Watch, match and nudge

3   **Practise, practise, practise.** Practise, make mistakes, practise, make mistakes, practise, make mistakes. This is the only way to learn – something we all found (often painfully) as children.

When can you use these How To*s?*

All the time.

What really happened in the corridor? If we go back to the conversation at the beginning of this chapter when three people met in the corridor, we can begin to understand the differences if we look at their gender.

You can also see that if each of them isn't practicing 'watch, match and nudge' then they will soon end up in 'shove'. This is when disaster begins to strike in any conversation.

Let me introduce the people again via the difference that surfaces in this conversation – their SHAPES, SHADES and SEX. Their key SHAPE is in bold.

- **Females:**   Yellow, Squiggle, **Triangle**, Blue
                  Violet, **Box**, Triangle, Blue
- **Male:**   Yellow, **Squiggle**, Triangle, Red

> *I just don't understand. Everything I do seems to have the opposite effect. I am working so hard at this relationship and it keeps going wrong.*

A Triangle, Box and Squiggle – and a male and two females. No wonder the conversation exploded!

Anger is a total communication breakdown – there is nothing constructive about becoming angry with someone, particularly in the situation shown above. But anger is a self directed thing, signalling frustration at failure to achieve your goal. Wouldn't it be good to be able to prevent the anger through targeted, empathic conversation?

The Great Divide – a really big gap

To understand the differences between the genders in this conversation there follows a breakdown of the conversation, separated into The Great Divide of SEX.

It is typical of millions of conversations in this new team-based environment where women now practice their version of communication at work with male partners who only know how to deal with them with their version.

The important thing is not the conversation itself. It is understanding what is going on behind it in people's heads. Once you know how to detect the issues, you can change your behavior. That is when you can begin to enjoy successful relationships.

Having successful relationships is just one of the personal benefits to the six Ss of personal success at work. From there the whole organization can benefit in so many different ways. Good communication affects just about everything that the organization does. So does bad communication.

What is just as important in this, and EVERY conversation, is what is going on in the (brackets) – in other words, in the speaker's head. And what is going on in the male or female heads is often TOTALLY different. Do you recognize the situation – and its outcomes?

The conversation broken down

Simply follow the numbers to follow the conversation.

Female

 Share

1

'Oh, by the way, can we get
together to talk about D?'
(I'm just fed up with everyone
going on about how little he
has done.)
'We need to agree where we
are going with him.'
(So we need to get together to
talk through the problem and
see what emerges.)

2

'Yes, that sounds good to me.'
(Every time Squiggle gets
involved in anything I lose
track. Perhaps he will talk over
his last conversation and share
what D said.)
'There are a number of
important points that need to
be worked out.'
(I have put a lot of work in and
before I do more I need to
know what is happening. I
know Squiggle had a meeting
with D; perhaps he can fill me
in on the detail.)

THE GREAT DIVIDE

Male

 Solve

3

'Great.'
(I bet they are going to tell me
what a great job I am doing,
getting all those alliances
going.)

At the meeting

 Share

1

'I'll kick off.' (I want to hear exactly what is going on here.)
'From what I can see we seem to be putting a lot in, and not getting as much out.'
(Squiggle works so hard to push this business forward – I don't want him messed about.)

3

'Each time we give more information away D seems to take it and not give us much credit.'
(There. That's given him the story.)

 Solve

2

(Hang on, they are frowning. This isn't the meeting I thought I was coming to. I'm not prepared for this. It seems pretty confrontational – and I have brought no notes.)
'OK, what are we going to do about it?'

4

(Oh, oh. She is being critical of me here, and her solution sounds as though she wants to stop the relationship with D.)
'Right.' (Let's see what solution they want – are they together on this?) 'What do you suggest we do?'

THE GREAT DIVIDE

5

(We really need to make a point here. We are wasting our time. Squiggle needs to know what is going on.)

'Recently he even quoted "ABC", our competitor, at a talk he was giving. He quoted them without even mentioning our work with him at all. Can you believe that!'

 Enhance/Exaggerate

 **Explain**

6

[*Getting annoyed*] (This is going too far. I am beginning to get fed up with this conversation already. It is all pretty damning stuff about my judgement. And we don't seem to get answers, only more problems – I can feel myself getting angry.)

'I get the message! What do you want me to do?'

(I'll try and justify myself here – they have me on the run.)

'I have been throwing him lots of ideas, to try to get him involved. I'm sure it will work out.'

(Come on, ladies, trust me here.)

7

(Why is he taking this so badly when he has done nothing wrong? We only wanted to let him know how we felt. Maybe if we emphasize the point here.)

'And do you know what really makes me angry? All that detailed work we conducted for our joint project is not being mentioned at all in another talk he is giving on the subject at a conference.'

T H E   G R E A T   D I V I D E

(That ought to convince him – now he knows the facts and how I feel.)

9

(Why does he keep taking this personally? I am just not getting across. Maybe if I back up Box it will help – she understands what I'm saying.)
'No, it's not your choice. What makes me so cross is that D seems to be taking advantage of us.'

T H E   G R E A T   D I V I D E

8

(Oh no, now they are mad and it looks like I've completely wasted my time – boy, do they think I've messed up. Yet I know I haven't.)
'Look, you seem to be suggesting I have made a bad choice here.'

10

[*Getting angry*] (I'm under attack here. This gets worse by the minute. Both of them are angry. They think D is really taking me for a ride. I'm mad with them for letting this get so far without telling me the situation. I'm mad with D for doing whatever he is not supposed to be doing. I'm mad with myself – and we still aren't actually sorting this out!)
'Right. You are saying all the time I've spent with D is totally wasted.'
(I'll throw in a solution here.)
I'll look for someone else to work with ...'
(No, that won't work, there is no-one else and it's not that bad anyway. I'd better back off this idea.)

Push/Pull

11

[*Trying to conciliate*] (Why is he taking this so personally? And now he's attacking us. I just don't know where to go with this conversation. How do I move it back to where I want it. I'll try and conciliate.)
'We are not suggesting anything drastic yet. We are just looking for a way to work effectively together for the future'.

12

[*Getting angry as well*] (I'm really trying to help here and he is pushing our help away. Well, I'm pushing back. I can dig my heels in when I want. In fact, I'm as angry as he is.)
'I simply wanted to show how each time we try working together we lose out. You are now suggesting I have failed to complete my work.'
(I sure am busy. I'm taking lots of work home. I'll let him know exactly how I feel here.)

T
H
E

G
R
E
A
T

D
I
V
I
D
E

'... but I don't see who we can go with.'
(And anyway, what the hell are these two doing about moving this forward?)
I know you have been busy but I don't see you two helping me on this. In fact the work you were supposed to help me do didn't get done.

 Order/Obey

'Everybody seems to be blaming everyone else and I'm not having it.'
(I can't cope with this conflict any more. Why is he doing this?)
'I'm going.'

13

'Don't go.' [Leaves to console Box]

10 minutes later – happy ending

 Share

2

(He's off again with another idea. We've already worked it out in the Ladies.)
'Thanks for letting us know how you feel.'

T H E G R E A T D I V I D E

14

(I'm really confused now. What a meeting. Why is this happening? I'm not blaming them. I'm just defending my position – can't they see they are challenging me?)
'I can't understand this. You are telling me I've really messed up and you are the ones now getting upset and leaving!'

 Solve

1

(I've just worked out what went wrong there. I'll let them know and apologize.)
'I'm sorry. Look, I know what happened. [Explains]'

3

'Don't worry, Squiggle, we go
back too long to let this affect us.
(We still haven't sorted this out.
Oh, well.)

4

(Good, that's that problem
sorted out. Now we can move
on.)
'Great, see you later.'

Summary – Sex at work

The story of the meeting in the corridor is just one example of the
thousand awkward positions males and females can, and do, get into
all the time!

With everyone's role changing, both male and female, we need to
identify what the underlying basics are between the sexes. It is critical to everyone in the new organizational structures they are working
in, to begin to think about where the communication styles of their
companies are heading. This is the basics of culture. Language, and
the way we work, create the climate (or what we experience) which in
turn creates the culture (or what we value).

The sex of organizations is changing – they are becoming both male
and female. Anyone who continues to work, male or female, in the
old male dominated, order/obey organization will not be utilizing
their own and the organization's abilities to the full. That would not
only be a shame, but is a waste of everyone's time and resources.

Before we look at how to use this knowledge to the full at the end of
the six Ss, try the following exercises.

Mental aerobic exercise no. 6:
He said – she said

Watch what happens when the two genders get together. Now you know what to look for, write down your observations.

You will be able to use these to play back to the people you are observing (provided they agree of course). You will also see how the opposites are just that, opposite. Whether you do anything about the gender difference by altering your style is now up to you.

Mental aerobic exercise no. 7:
She said to him – and he said to her

She needs to write him an e-mail, or even talk to him face to face. She knows what she wants to do and she wants him to feel some ownership of the answer. How does she do it? Prepare what you would do in her shoes. Bear in mind 'he' likes to solve problems, explain the facts and either to be ordering or obeying, depending on the 'pecking order'.

Next reverse the situation. He talks to her. She likes to share, enhance the facts for effect ('Oh no I would never, ever do that!') and does not need to order or obey, but to feel that the other person is pulling the relationship closer, not pushing it apart.

It doesn't matter who is boss. What is important is that each uses the gender language of the other.

E-mail to: Him/Her

Subject:

From: Her/Him

SENSES – THE FOURTH S OF SUCCESS

How do you experience life?

How does the way you see what happens, hear what happens and feel what happens affect everything you do?

Appealing to people's SENSES will get you closer to them than you can ever imagine.

Senses

What is this chapter about?

We learn all about our world by taking in information with our eyes, ears, touch, taste and smell. This chapter helps you understand how people use their SENSES to understand and explain the world around them. You will discover what lies beneath the surface when people say ...

'I see what you mean.' 'I hear what you say.' 'I feel this makes sense.'

How you benefit – the hooks

Once you know how people absorb information, and how they express themselves you will automatically know which way they prefer to have things expressed to them.

It's called 'targeting' in marketing and 'rapport' in everyday life. Once you know how to target or gain rapport you will get people on your side more easily.

You will gain most by ...

... worrying less about the jargon and actually trying out the basic concepts for yourself. The section at the end gives you more ideas on how to apply your knowledge in the real world.

Senses

Anyone who is in marketing or selling uses their SENSES to see, hear and feel what is going on and to express their message. Before they can do this they need to sell themselves by using the right words, pace, tone, expressions, body language and emotions. They will also have identified the habits that they think are more likely to help them succeed in influencing others.

Those involved in advertising use their knowledge of what motivates people to create visions that make others want to 'buy in' to the dream they have created.

Advertising tries to appeal to your SENSES. How? Through visual, auditory and feeling sensations. Advertising uses pictures, sounds, taste and touch. These images, sounds, etc. appeal to your senses through the language they use.

Our fourth S, SENSES, shows the power behind the language of marketing and selling. Once again, if we understand why things happen and what works best we can then begin to change behavior as a result.

People power

Think about why clubs are so popular. People like people who are like themselves and like the things they like. Obvious, isn't it? And it's a real breakthrough into another dimension of understanding people.

When you WATCH people, then you can make yourself speak and act like them as you MATCH yourselves to them.

Jingles sell, jingles sell – adverts all the day

Once they see, hear or feel that you are like them then they will like you. You can then begin to NUDGE them into buying into your ideas, suggestions and recommendations.

This is the basis of what we call 'rapport'.

Rapport and the Watch, Match and Nudge Model

You think this	I think and do this	Watch, match, nudge
1 You are interested in yourself and you think ... 'I like what I say and do.'	2 I am interested in you and I think ... 'I like being with you. I'll really watch and listen.'	3 I WATCH YOU By listening, observing and asking you about yourself (PS. I don't have to agree with what you say!)
4 You are showing you like me by listening, and you think ... 'I like people who listen to what I say and do.'	5 I am showing I like you by thinking ... 'I'm interested in you. So I show you I'm interested in what you say and do. How? I play back what you say and do.'	6 I MATCH YOU By saying, doing and acting just like you.
7 I'm ready to be influenced because ... 'I like you. You are my sort of person. I'd really like to know more about you, and what you have to offer.'	8 I like you and I like to show it so I help you and I tempt you with a language you are now ready for, e.g. 'You might find this interesting/ exciting/useful ... etc.'	9 I NUDGE YOU I begin to influence you by finding out what you want and need and put my ideas in a way that you want to buy.

Now you can see why learning about the SENSES (and the other five Ss as well) is such a good idea – it is a win–win for everyone. You get what you want and the other person gets what they want. And you do it without having to resort to high pressure selling techniques.

If you don't know what to look for or listen to, in order to be able to get close to people, how can you possibly begin to influence them?

This model is used in sales situations. Once again the steps are critical when trying to get deep into someone else's psyche.

The sales model to changing behavior:

| **Establish** | **Watch** |
| **Need** | By observing what they say, do and want. |

Establish	**Match**
Features &	By telling what the product does and showing what
Benefits	you get out of it.

"
Just sign here,
Madam.
"

Close the	**Nudge**
Sale	By influencing them to part with their money, or even
	buy two, through using sales techniques.

It doesn't stop there.

Everybody has models of changing behavior.

You didn't get where you are today without doing something right. We are all pretty good at influencing people. Here is one example of the way we affect other people through what we say and do:

"
Daddy, can I have
one of those?
Please can I? Can
I? Can I? Please
… thanks.
"

'Hello! Nice to meet you.'	**Watch** This is called phatic communicating, all those *hellos* and chit chat.
'They didn't do that, did they? That's awful.'	**Match** This is called cathartic communication. People let off steam as they agree with how 'bad' things are. This is one type of matching.
'It would have been better if ...'	**Nudge** This is called influencing communication

Getting to know you – from head to toe

A particular method of personal effectiveness that strongly focuses on SENSES is Neuro Linguistic Programming (NLP). NLP focuses on Neuro (the senses), Linguistic (the language) and Programming (the behavior).

"I just hate these TLAs"*

*Three letter acronyms

A course in NLP would help you, but will take you many weeks or months and quite a lot of money to become a Master Practitioner. Here, for quick reference, is my KISS model of one of the key elements of NLP – rapport.

Called the Head to Toe model, it allows you to sweep down from top to toe and remember what to look and listen for – in an order that is easy to remember.

Once you know what to look and listen for you can start to Watch, Match and Nudge. Creating rapport is critical if you are going to influence people.

The Head to Toe model

Head   Watch how they hold it

Expressions   Watch the ones they make, especially eyebrows

Ears   How much are they listening?

Eyes   Do they look up, to the side or down?

Words   Boxy, squiggly, triangle, circle, male, female

Voice   High/low

                  Fast/slow

                  Quiet/loud

                  Pauses/no pauses

Gestures   Open, fast, considered, careful, sweeping

Posture   Closed down, arms crossed, legs crossed, hunched,
                  proud, open, attentive, leaning forward, filling up
                  the space.

> *I love this body language. It's so intimate!*

Simple, isn't it? And the beauty is you do it ALL THE TIME. You are observing the Head to Toe model every time you meet people. The problem is, are you operating on YOUR model of them or are you taking a fresh approach and using THEIR model? Here is what to look and listen out for. I call it 'If not – guess what'. If you watch, and don't match – guess what? The nudge won't happen.

We've already covered many of the words people use with our look at SHAPES, SHADES and SEX. There are lots of books on body language so let's concentrate on just a few of the headlines!

If Not – Guess What

Head

Does the person you are watching cock their head to one side, showing their interest? If they do then are you showing your interest too?

If not, guess what?

If you are not on their wavelength that's where the mismatch occurs.

Expressions

Watch their face, especially the eyebrows, they are the real give-away. Are they frowning? Are they worried? Are you?

If not, guess what?

If they are unhappy and you appear the opposite or different that's when the mismatch occurs.

Ears

How much are they listening? Are you talking too much? Do you ask them 'What do you think of it so far?' Are you doing all the talking and not listening?

If not, guess what?

One way communication is usually not communication, it is a monologue.

One thing leads to another (I SEE what you mean!)

We all use sensory specific language and this is the clue to identifying a person's dominant form of communication – seeing, hearing or touching. If you are a visual person, what you see is the most important thing that influences you. So, as a predominantly SEEING person you will live your life seeing pictures and images.

Because your perceptions are so visually oriented, guess what? You like describing what happens to you by using pictures and images. Most of all you use visual words – like 'see' and 'look' and 'picture'.

The words below are the words and phrases in the language of Visual people. Visual people will say things like:

'I **can picture** the **scene**.'
'Can we take this from a different **view**?'
'There is a problem I **see** coming up on the **horizon**.'

"
This stuff makes me see red.
"

If Visual people use Visually based words, and you don't – guess what? You won't get on with them as well as you might!

If you match your words to theirs, you are more likely to appeal to their visual way of expressing themselves. Language expresses what people think but it also gives away what they are like.

I HEAR what you are saying!

Just as Visual people work in pictures and images, HEARING people operate in sounds and conversations. They use words associated with sound to express themselves:

"
Hear ye. Hear ye.
"

'I **hear** what you are saying.'
'How does that **sound** to you?'
'**Listen**, I want you to **ring** someone up for me.'

If you then talk in their auditory language they will form better relationships with you.

I can GRASP this easily!

Now you have got the picture and have listened to what I am saying, no doubt you will have grasped this new approach.

If you are a TOUCHING person you will think and talk using words with strong kinaesthetic associations, like:

> Deep down I believe this has some powerful applications.

'Don't **hit** me with this news again.'
' I **feel** this won't work.'
' I have a **gut reaction** this will succeed.'

I feel you have got the hang of all this. So here is a chart that lays all of this out in a simple list. How does it look to you? Do the phrases sound right? Do you connect with the sense of it all?

SENSES – the language chart

Seeing people (Visual)	Hearing people (Auditory)	Feeling people (Kinaesthetic)
I **see** what you are saying.	I **hear** what you are saying.	I can **grasp** this easily.
This **looks** familiar.	This **sounds** familiar.	This **feels** familiar.
Are we **seeing** the same thing?	Are we **singing** off the same hymn sheet?	Do we **feel** the same way?
The **light** has come on.	That **rings** a bell.	This **touches** a nerve.
It **looks** OK to me.	**Sounds** fine.	My **gut reaction** is it will work.
Have you got the **picture**?	Are we on the same **wavelength**?	Can we **touch** base again on this?
I didn't **notice** anything.	I never **heard** a word.	I never **felt** frightened.
You are a **sight** for sore eyes.	This is **music** to my **ears.**	That **turns** me on.
Hmm. I **see**!		

Sometimes it may be quite difficult to distinguish whether people are SEEING, HEARING or FEELING. However the chances are that they will have one main sense they rely on and that they will have a secondary sense they use as well.

What do you do when faced with this dilemma? Paul McKenna, the leading UK hypnotist and exponent of NLP, has an interesting way of working with people. What does he do when he is hypnotising them? He hedges his bets! He uses words in all of the key SENSES to make sure he hooks into the person he is talking to. Here is how he does it when hypnotising someone;

'I want you to imagine a scene where you are being successful. I want you to really see what you see, hear what you hear, feel what you feel. Now I want you to magnify the sensations, make what you see stronger, what you hear louder and what you feel more powerful.'

If it's good enough for a leading hypnotist, who is also a leading light in NLP, then it's good enough for me!

So here is the word chart. These are the most powerful words that appeal to each of the SENSES. Your best bet is to use them all to achieve buy-in. This will work very well for you when you are presenting to groups of people, as you are bound to get a mixture of SENSES anyway.

More clues:

SEEING – eyes looking UP

HEARING – eyes looking SIDEWAYS

FEELING – eyes looking DOWN.

"
See me, feel me,
touch me, heal me.
"

Tommy, The Who

This looks/sounds/feels good

Senses – some of the power words

Seeing – EYES UP

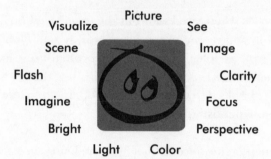

Picture

Visualize   See

Scene   Image

Flash   Clarity

Imagine   Focus

Bright   Perspective

Light   Color

Hearing – EYES SIDEWAYS

Noise   Listen

Sound   Hear

Crash   Groan

Chord   Chat

Ring   Bang

Say   Harmony

Wavelength   Tune

Talk Music

Feeling – EYES DOWN

Cold   Rough

Touch   Smooth

Push   Hot

Solid   Grasp

Feel   Tackle

Grab   Firm

Struck

Remember, the power of images, sound, smells and touch can have a profound impact on what we think, feel, believe, say and do.

To all of you marketeers out there, this must sound pretty familiar. To all those of you who aren't, just look, sniff and feel the next time you are watching an advert or buying a product. Isn't this what marketing is supposed to do? Getting your senses going is what makes you buy. If this isn't the purpose of every advert, promotion and sales encounter then they aren't doing their job!

> *50% of advertising works – I just don't know which 50%.*

Marketing people know about, and use the power of visual images, sound, music, jingles, repeated words and phrases, taste, touch and smell. The market is split into what marketing people call segments; different groups of consumers with different needs and requirements. If these methods of attracting us using the SENSES are not aimed, or targeted at us, we won't want to buy the product. If they are, we will!

This is all well and good, you might be thinking. But I am not in marketing. Oh yes you are. And the single most important product or service that you will ever market is YOU. You are Me Inc. or Me plc.

Now we come to the crunch. Do you really buy-in to what you are, what you could be and what you need to do to make the most of this incredible product called YOU?

This is where NLP does a wonderful job. It allows you to learn how to build yourself into whatever you want to be. Once you have developed this product called YOU it then gives you all the tools of the trade to market yourself to everyone else.

How does it do this? By getting you to examine where you have been, where you are, and where you want to be. Once you have decided all three NLP sets about showing you how other successful people achieved their success and how you can emulate them. The steps look something like this:

Three steps to heaven

The before and after steps

Step 1

Here is where you are/were (before)

Step 2

Here is where you could be (after)

Step 3

This is what you could do to get there – both internally and externally, by using NLP models of best behaviors (during)

Just as marketing creates adverts to get you to 'buy', so NLP gets you to create your own personal adverts – featuring you. You can go as far as you like in creating some compelling ways of getting the message across to yourself. It's called creating your personal vision.

Once you have your new pictures of the future you, then you can make the leap into doing things differently. Do things differently and you will soon discover you will get what you want. To help you get there through the help of others, NLP shows you how to target your new message to your audience as well.

The difference between NLP and marketing is that marketing is based on developing and communicating messages about external products and services. NLP is about YOU as the product that you want to develop.

And the great thing is that you can use so many tools available to excite the SENSES and emotions.

NLP taps into the subconscious things that makes us behave the way we do.

It uses concepts like visualization, that is imagining what you want in your mind's eye.

NLP also uses verbal instructions like affirmations, repeating messages to yourself – goals or statements of intent that you keep in your mind. It does all this to get you talking to yourself and imagining what life might be like. Why? Because words have power and this has an impact on your psychology – it unleashes on you the power of your own mind.

NLP also shows people how to learn through the world of stories and anecdotes, called 'metaphors'.

Once upon a time ...

A lot of this is just what marketing does!

To make things simpler, and to bring all of these concepts together, we have developed a new brand name encompassing NLP and the other five Ss. We call it **inter-relationship marketing**. It is about how you market YOU, and how everyone markets themselves to all their customers, colleagues, stakeholders and suppliers! So here is a quick foray into a new concept for you to play with.

Inter-relationship marketing

Marketing to customers works on what is popularly known as the four Ps. These are product, place, price, and promotion. It's called the marketing mix. Product is what you make, place is where you want to sell it, price is the amount of money you want to charge, and promotion is the way you encourage awareness of your product. To make things easy we have used similar descriptions in our concept of inter-relationship marketing.

The four *P*s of marketing YOU

Product   You! Your skills, ability, capability, body, mind.

Packaging   How you look; the way you dress, your body lan-
                guage. How you put yourself across to others. For
                example with enthusiasm, passion, humor, seri-
                ousness, formality, informality, etc.

Promotion   What you say and do to influence other people.
                How you get others to buy into you and how you
                change what they think and do about you and oth-
                ers.

Principles The concepts you live by which help you or drive
                you to think and do things differently and to influ-
                ence others behavior. These are your values, vision,
                mission and goals.

Perfect Promotions Produce Passionate Purchasers

Marketing has created strategies, processes and tools to help organizations develop their products and services for customers. NLP has
also developed the same kind of concepts which can be used for
ordinary people. It makes sense to put the lessons learned from
marketing together with the lessons learned from NLP – which is
what we are doing with the six Ss.

The lesson for today

Does all this talk of marketing and NLP sound like the latest in modern thinking? Before moving on to STATUS it is worth leaving you
with a few words from one of the greatest team of NLP practitioners
of all time, Paul, one of the twelve disciples.

Why choose someone from the Bible to describe an apparently modern phenomenon? After explaining a recent breakthrough in these learning techniques to a very wise vicar, he firmly and kindly reminded me that a much greater being had developed, and given man the techniques a long time before the 'discovery' we know today. He pointed out that Jesus and his disciples were practising NLP 2000 years before anyone even thought of the name.

ACTS 28:31
Paul preaches at Rome under guards

The Holy Spirit **spoke** the truth to your forefathers when he said through the prophet Isiah
'**Go** to these people and say,
You will be ever **hearing**, but never understanding.
You will be ever **seeing** but never perceiving.
For this people's **heart** has become calloused:
they hardly **hear** with their **ears**,
and they have closed their **eyes**.
Otherwise they might **see** with their **eyes**
hear with their ears,
understand with their **hearts**,
and **turn**, and **I would lead them**.

No wonder they let Paul walk freely, even though he was under arrest. He had appealed to them all, in a way they all understood – the visual – seeing, the auditory – hearing, and the kinaesthetic – going, turning, leading. Powerful stuff, and nobody had taught him NLP or marketing. It was there all the time.

Paul's STATUS as a prisoner didn't make a scrap of difference to him. I wonder if that is true in your organization. We will look at STATUS next. Which reminds me of a wonderful story:

A junior manager went to her director and said:
'I am doing the job of the next person above me, please can I have the title Senior Manager?'
The Director smiled knowingly and benignly said
'I know you are doing a great job, and that is all that matters, titles are not important.'
To which the junior manager replied
'Well you won't mind if I have yours then?'

Does STATUS matter? Find out after your mental aerobics on SENSES!

Mental aerobic exercise no. 8:
I see what you are saying

Write down some of the expressions that you hear people using when they are in Visual, Auditory or Kinaesthetic (feeling) mode.

You will be able to see how to use them in future as you begin to get more of a handle on how SENSE will work best for you.

Look into my eyes!

Visual expressions

	WHO	says	WHAT
Name	_____		_____
Name	_____		_____
Name	_____		_____

Auditory expressions

Name	_____	_____
Name	_____	_____
Name	_____	_____

Kinaesthetic expressions

Name	_____	_____
Name	_____	_____
Name	_____	_____

Mental aerobic exercise no. 9:
Show me how you feel

You want to know if someone is Visual, Auditory or Kinaesthetic. How do you find out? Get them to tell you a story. The two topics below will give them lots of opportunity to use their favored language. Listen to their words. Make notes. Being interested is going to make your relationship stronger anyway. Everyone loves a good listener!

Story 1

Imagine you have so much money you can buy any luxury item you like, for example a car. Describe it. What do you like best about it? Tell me what you would do with it. (e.g. I would buy an old Jaguar XJS. It's **sleek**, **feels** great to drive, the inside **smells** terrific. I can **see myself** driving down the road in the sun. The wind **feels good** in my hair ...)

Story 2

What would be your favorite job and why? (e.g. I would love to be the creative head of an advertising agency. I would design adverts with plenty of **colorful** and **wacky images**. I can **picture** the sort of ads I would come up with for TV ...)

Mental aerobic exercise no. 10:
It makes Sense to me

You are about to introduce a new product or service into your range. The implications of introducing this new product are that EVERYONE in the organization will be affected by it. Whether it's Customer Services who must design some new forms, or Packing who need to build new racks, everyone is involved.

So how do you target everyone?

Describe the benefits to the whole company of introducing this new idea. Write it in a way that everyone will relate to.

e.g.

New fresh tasty red Whizzo

You will all soon be **seeing** a new **colorful** leaflet, and **listening to** and **watching** a new video on the launch of New Whizzo. We all sometimes **feel** that new ideas can add more work to our crazy schedules. **Deep down** you all know, however, we can't **stand** still. **Watch** what our competitors are doing. They will **sniff** out any weaknesses in our range. Now is the time for us to **grit our teeth** and **put** our best foot forward ...

(OK. So it's over the top. See if you can do better.)

STATUS – THE FIFTH S OF SUCCESS

How does your upbringing affect what you say and do?

How does your STATUS at work affect what you say and do?

What happens to communication in a 'flat' structure?

What happens when we bring our childhood into the work place

How abolishing the business hierarchy and working in teams changes our communication – completely!

Status

What is this chapter about?

We learned a lot as kids. We practised how to become adults. We learned a script from our parents for dealing with all those every-day things like dealing with other people, and dealing with life. The trouble was it often was the wrong script! Our rules on STATUS learned at home as kids affect how we operate at work as adults. The trouble is we often still act as the kids we were.

At work we learned a lot from 'experts' (the supervisors and managers) who taught us how to act and behave. We learned about management, leadership, hierarchy, boss and subordinate relationships, deferring to authority and how to work in an order and obey system run by men. Then someone threw out the rules. We now live and work in a 'downsized', 'empowered', 'multi-skilled', egalitarian system where women are (increasingly) as much in charge. We are all learning a new set of rules about our STATUS at work.

How you benefit

Discovering how we learned our behavior under the old regimes as kids and as adults in a 'top down' structure at work will show how we are conditioned to act under certain circumstances. Once you know about this conditioning you can learn how to deal with it.

You will gain most by ...

... thinking about how you have been 'conditioned'. Ask yourself if you still throw tantrums like a child if you don't get your own way, or don't speak up for fear of upsetting the boss. Now watch how other people are acting. Once again, when you get the measure of them you will be able to target your message to get understanding and commitment, and not a tantrum! At the end of the chapter are more methods for applying the theories to real life examples.

Status: who's boss at home and at work?

- Ingredient number one – your STATUS at home in your family (and how you bring it into work)
- Ingredient number two – your STATUS at work (and guess what? You take it home!)

Ingredient number one – status at home

With no other role models besides the ones that you grew up with, the way you behaved at home and hence your relationship with your family were instilled in you at a very early age. It is not surprising that later in life we employ the same reactions, thoughts, words and deeds that we learned when we were little.

The theory behind how our influences as a child affect our behavior as adults is called *Transactional Analysis* (TA), originated by Dr Eric Berne. Summed up it means:

Transactions what we say and how we say it when we talk with others

Analysis the job of psychiatrists – if we can understand what is happening, we can start to put it right!

TA is excellent for helping us understand how we take our behavior from childhood into adulthood.

The three modes of Transactional Analysis (TA) are called Parent, Adult and Child (PAC)

Parent

The holder of life's traditions and values, given to you in the first five years of your life. The recordings of what was said and done during these years remain with you to re-say and re-enact whenever we think we should get into 'tell' mode. A Parent is filled with **demands, directions and dogma**.

Adult

The adult **reasons, thinks, predicts and figures out how to** do things. This is the Vulcan in us, the logical, analytical questioning Mr Spock in Star Trek who reacts to reason.

Child

The responses to what the parent said or did. They are the feelings we felt when, as children, we were cornered, dependent, unfairly accused, clumsy or uninformed. Confronted in adult life we play the old tapes again.

When free to be so, the child can be **inventive, creative and spontaneous**. But it becomes a problem part of our personality if **fearful, intimidated or selfish**.

> *If you think you are going to get me doing that you won't, won't, won't – so there.*

When is TA useful?

> *I'm not OK, you're not OK, but that's OK!*

There's a lot we can learn from in TA, particularly in terms of understanding what makes us tick. How we behave at work is frequently a reflection of what we learned from our STATUS when we were young, as the following three examples illustrate.

Don't treat me this way!

1 Sue was in a meeting and objected to the way it was heading. Suddenly, without prior warning or hesitation, she shouted at everyone in the room, and stormed out. Now, what does that behavior remind you of – a spoilt child perhaps?

2 One (slightly older) manager was offering what he thought was reasoned, impartial advice to another colleague. The person on the receiving end suddenly exclaimed: 'Don't you patronize me!'. The manager's fatherly tone was rejected in a somewhat petulant, childlike way.

3 A young, bright but relatively new recruit to an organization was presenting a report to the Chairman, who thought it was excellent. Then he came across a part he did not understand and, despite several attempts at an explanation, he still remained confused. Perhaps his tone reminded her of a teacher or adult in her childhood, or he came across as being in 'parent' mode. Whatever the cause, she went into 'child' mode and burst out crying.

When faced with a similar script to the one you learned as a child, your behavior may well seem to be caught in a time warp and, suddenly, you are the person you were then. The child in you explodes and storms out of the room muttering, or even screaming 'Nobody loves me, I am never going to speak to you again!' Or the child who is now an adult reacts to someone playing 'parent' with 'Don't you patronize me!'

PAC – it's easy as 123

Inside each of us is the Parent, the Adult and the Child.

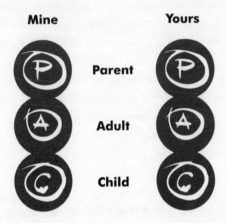

Everything is fine if the part of me talking to you is in harmony with the part of you talking to me, as shown in the following transactions.

Complementary transactions

Adult to Adult – this will go OK

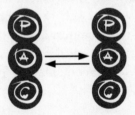

'Have you heard about the downsizing happening in the organization?'.

'Yes, it's going to mean a lot of redundancies'.

Parent to Parent – this is OK too

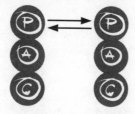

'Just as I thought. Those idiots on the board have announced more redundancies.'

'I wouldn't have expected anything less of that lot. I bet they have looked after their own backsides.'

'Yes and probably given themselves a raise as well.'

Child to Child – and this is OK

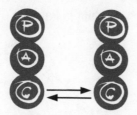

'Oh my God have you heard about the frightening number of layoffs? I feel sick just thinking about what I will do if I get kicked out.'

'I hadn't heard. Nobody tells me anything. I'm livid. I am going to give my boss a piece of my mind. You would have thought the old fool would have spoken to me.'

Different yet complementary modes

Parent to Child

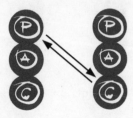

'Now Mary don't be upset but I have to let you know that you're going to have to cut out all these telephone calls to your girl-friends on company time. It just won't do.'

'Oh come on Mr Smith you know me – I wouldn't take advantage of you would I?'

Child to Parent

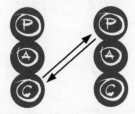

'Will everyone just let me get on with this? I am fed up with so many interruptions.'

'Well if you weren't so busy on things you shouldn't be doing then you wouldn't have to shout.'

Non-complementary transactions

Parent to Child – Adult responds

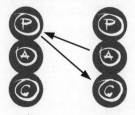

'Why are you bothering with that?'

'This is a report I am finishing which will help the department gain greater efficiency.'

You may be asking yourself what has this got to do with personal success at work? The answer is quite simple. It is only by understanding how people operate, where their behavior originates and where you can predict their behavior might go, that you can begin to avoid the transactions which are not constructive and damaging to communication.

Transactional Analysis – personal traits, company cultures

TA covers many different approaches to handling transactions. Made popular in *I'm OK – You're OK* by Thomas A. Harris, It also creates an understanding of our personality, giving us the ability to look at and comprehend why we behave the way we do. The approach to dealing with others when they are in one of the Parent, Adult, Child modes is a useful marketing tools to add to your learning of how we communicate at work.

Whole organizations are acting in Parent mode.

Here are some of the personality types and tools you can use to describe individual people. Interestingly the descriptions apply to individuals, as well as whole organizations. What is significant about the types they describe is the different use of language which falls under each category. For example, in a very Parent oriented situation you are likely to find a very 'tell' mode of communication. Both the verbal and body language will be similar to the role of parent. Watch out for the corporate video with 'Dad' the Chairman smiling proudly at his 'children' throughout the company. Just listen to the number of times he says 'We must do this. We must do that. We must do the other.' It sounds like my parents – does it yours?

By listening and watching the way other people behave, and the way you behave, you will see personality traits of Parent, Adult and Child coming through your own, other people's, and whole organizations' ways of behaving. The most obvious ones might be:

- Parent as an individual – a benign or autocratic boss
- Parent as an organization, e.g. traditional manufacturing or one of the old financial institutions
- Adult as an individual – cool, calm considered professional like a doctor
- Adult as an organization, e.g. hospital, lawyers
- Child as an individual – happy go lucky creative sort like a designer
- Child as an organization, e.g. advertising agency.

Ingredient number two – status at work

Just like the other techniques already described under SHAPES, SHADES, SEX and SENSES, the techniques of TA as a way of understanding status can be fused together to help you communicate better with others. So too the rules of dealing with people in the hierarchy at work can be used to everyone's benefit.

If people like to be listened to, and the manager just likes giving people a 'good talking to' then it is not hard to see that there is a pretty big mismatch occurring. Understanding the rules will create a win–win situation.

The four golden rules of STATUS at work and the implications on communication

Golden rule 1 – top down: some people like to lead and some people like to be led

Some people like to lead and give direction, create motivation and have their ideas and desires fulfilled by others working for and with them. Other people like to be led. They cannot 'see' into the future, have no desire to tell others what they want doing and are content to act on others instructions or direction. This is where vision and mission statements are useful. They are usually created by those who like to lead, to give direction and help those who don't.

Great rule, but how does it fit in the new global, team-based environment? How does it fit where every individual is in charge of themselves because organizations have 'empowered' them to get on with it? The answer is that this is the new dichotomy. If you empower individuals, how do you then get them to take the lead from someone else?

What makes this problem worse is that in a recent survey it was found that people in organizations did not believe their senior management.

64% ...
of employees do not believe their senior management

Put this another way – two-thirds of people say that their senior management are LIARS! This is an appalling statistic, but is it surprising? After all the downsizing, redundancies and massive programs of restructuring too many people feel that their managers cannot or will not give them true information. So even if they communicate, no-one listens.

Only 6% of companies feel that they have had any measurable level of success with programs to instill corporate vision, missions and values.

Yet people like to have strong leadership. And the leaders like to lead. If they are to do their job how do they do it? And how is it affecting them if they feel they are not getting through?

The way that true leaders do this is simple. They have a new 'deal' to get through to the people who are looking for that leadership. The deal is this:

'I will listen to your needs, if you listen to mine'

This puts leadership in a new light. No longer can people with responsibility over others in the organization afford to be in the old 'tell' mode.

The only way that leaders can communicate and get people to take their messages on board is to influence them to 'buy'.

How do leaders communicate in the new age of empowerment and sophisticated internal audiences?

- Successful leaders now treat people like their customers.
- They find out their needs.
- They listen to their concerns.
- They match what they want to do with the needs of others.
- They communicate with people in their language.
- They target their message in a way that generates excitement, even passion.

Does this sound familiar? We call it internal marketing.

The new model of strong leadership is a two-way commitment to top down AND bottom up.

So any focus on the new STATUS of leaders who must communicate 'top down' must now be on golden rule no. 2 'Bottom up'.

Golden rule 2 – bottom up: people like to be listened to.

Everyone, everywhere likes to be listened to. They might like strong leadership, but no one is happy about being treated like a stuffed dummy. Listening is the key to understanding and gaining commitment from others. Treating people with the respect they all deserve, whoever they are and whatever they do is critical to their self esteem and motivation.

The new mode of listening sits alongside the realization that managers can no longer control people in organizations. This is why empowerment and the handing down of responsibility is more than nice to have, it is inevitable. The way to get things done is to let people get on with it.

What does this mean for the STATUS of the people who used to be 'lower down'? Suddenly there is no real lower down!

Everyone is important, and they know it. Telling them what to do is a thing of the past. People want respect, and they are demanding it! If in your organization they aren't demanding respect and being listened to, they soon will.

The concept of feedback and acting on feedback is not just fashionable, it is critical. This is exactly the same as what external customers expect. If you don't listen to their needs, they go elsewhere. They know it, they're exposed to it everywhere and they bring this ethic with them into the work place.

The time has come to change the way that organizations communicate, because the people in the organizations, and the organization itself has changed.

Hooray – and up she rises

Listening by the organization is one of many answers. If your new STATUS is important then you have a job to do as well. You have a responsibility to communicate upwards too. If you want to be heard, you have to market yourself, and market your message. If you don't, somebody else will. And if they are in competition with you for the next project, place on a team, promotion or even a job, then how you market yourself will be vital to your future.

Old organizational theory used to focus on the 'manager', they were the ones who were trained. Now everyone is a manager, of themselves.

When it comes to how you are seen by everyone in the organization you are the brand manager of YOU.

Your new found STATUS puts you in charge. The new tools of technology, like the Internet and internal Web sites, and some of the new methods of verbal feedback like Team Listening™ and hotlines, allow you to say your piece. And if you decide not to say your piece. If you say your piece and you don't target your message properly, then you will be in as much trouble as the senior managers who find two thirds of people don't believe them.

The teamwork and co-operation here is amazing.

Marketing yourself upwards is vital to grab a piece of the action and be involved in what is going on. Communicating with everyone else in the organization so that the job gets done is probably even more important. It is in side-to-side communication that you will be seen to add value and make a contribution. This will be a great decider of your future in the organization.

Golden rule 3 – side to side – people like to make a positive contribution

Most people want to make a positive contribution to their organization – they want to add value. When this happens they like to be recognized by their colleagues (not just their boss) for their efforts. How is it that people add value? They do their job and then they do more. Total Quality, best practice, business process re-engineering, innovation and a thousand and one 'initiatives' that organizations do, mean that everyone can contribute by doing something, or sometimes everything, in a new or different way.

The new STATUS of everyone in the organization is to be involved in Change.

Everyone is affected somehow, in some way by this thing called Change. Even Change has changed, it has now got a capital letter as it is so important.

You will be expected to change, and be a driver of Change. That makes you an important person.

> Getting through to other departments is worse than trying to push water uphill.

How you change, how you work with others as they change, how you get people to buy-in to your improvements and ideas will be critical to your success and that of your organization. Your ability to be an effective communicator with everyone at work will ensure your success. How do you do that? You repeat the same things that the leaders are doing.

- You treat people as your customers.
- You find out their needs.
- You listen to their concerns.
- You match what they want to do with your needs.
- You communicate with people in their language.
- You target your message in a way that generates excitement, even passion.

> I give all my business to them. I just think they CARE about me.

Democracy rules OK

Once you have this mastered, then you can start to work on those people who have an even more important STATUS in your organization. They are the people OUTSIDE your organization.

Golden rule 4 – inside out: this covers everyone outside work.

You may be doing a great job. Now ask yourself, is your organization making a difference to its customers and the community at large – the now fashionable 'stakeholders'?

Most people like to know that what they are doing actually makes a difference. They want to make a difference to the stakeholders involved in their work, be they customers, the community, shareholders, suppliers or strategic alliances. The same is true of those people looking from the outside in. Their STATUS has changed radically in the last 50 or so years. No longer are governments and industry the prime drivers. Individuals are – individuals as customers, consumers, as part of the local community, as part of a global community, as pressure groups, as shareholders, as parents, as voters, as institutional investors, as independent non-executive directors, as influencers, as pensioners, as past employees, as trade unionists, as strategic partners, as the press, as letter writers to the papers, as Internet newsgroups, as interactive TV subscribers, as tax payers, as benefit claimers, as paramilitary groups, as expatriates ... the list goes on, and it gets more fragmented every day.

Every one of these groups has a new STATUS and can influence your business. Two things then transpire. How they communicate with, to, at, for or against you will be important. How your organization, and EVERY INDIVIDUAL in it communicates with them will be important too. The interesting thing is that you belong to quite a few of the groups looking in on organizations. It is YOU who now has the power to influence, both ways.

Why are these four golden rules important to me?

- Top down
- Bottom up
- Side to side
- Inside out

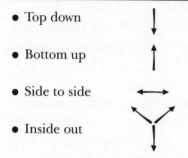

Communication from you to each of these groups is critical as they ALL now have a new STATUS.

Three directions of communication – inside and out

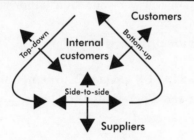

The diagram 'The Six Directions of Communication – Inside and Out' shows a lot more than simple arrows. It shows the new way organizations are conducting business. Job titles, hierarchy, bosses, subordinates, instructions, memos and all the accoutrements of the old hierarchy are going.

STATUS is a shared concept in today's organization, titles can mean nothing and bosses are being seen as no more important than their colleagues. The question we should address is 'What does this mean for you and me?' Your new STATUS comes from YOU and how well you can market yourself and your ideas to others.

Me Inc. Me plc Me Ltd Me & Co.

Your new STATUS is Me Inc.

You are the best person to market yourself and what you can offer. The rewards are great: success in attaining the goals you want from life.

YOU are the product, you can market yourself, and get people to want to buy. You are the service that provides your customers – who will pay good money – with the things they need to succeed.

Your customer is also the people all around you, because if you don't promote yourself, show others your best, and deliver what they ask of you, how can they deliver the goods to their customers?

You could be a factory worker, technology expert, boss or secretary; in addition to your core skills you must be able to get across to others your ideas and your contribution to the organization. If you don't, then somebody else will, and your contribution won't be recognized!

We are heading towards a new era. The era of 'Me Inc.'

You have a new STATUS, that of Chairman, Chief Executive, Marketing Director and Operations Director of 'Me Inc.'

Your STATUS now – a status check of everything so far in this new business of yours

STATUS at home and at work have given us a view of the influences on our lives from our position in the family and within the community at work. We know how we are likely to react in a given situation.

We have also covered our work style with SHADES, our attitudes with SHAPES and the gender influences on us with SEX. We then looked at how our SENSES affect the way we 'see' our world.

Now is the time for a reminder of how all this adds up to give us a view on the things we say, do, think and feel about the things going on in our business lives. This is our status check for everything going on, in, and around Me Inc.

If we are to mobilize hearts and minds at work by stirring others' emotions, we do this by understanding the psycho graphics and demographics of the people we deal with. This is what the Six S's is all about.

Understanding people is the starting point of all marketing. From this understanding we can move to generating the emotions that stir people into action. The most powerful of these is passion. Before we go on, to show how to generate passion we need to understand what passion is. So here are a number of questions you might ask about this most powerful emotion – passion.

- What are people passionate about?
- How passionate are they about it?
- How deep does it run?
- What do they do differently as a result of feeling strongly about things?
- Does it show?
- Can it be measured?
- Can it be transferred to others?

Once you have this piece of market research, then you are really ready to start crafting and targeting your messages. But which messages? Try the following tick list to see what you want people to be passionate about in your business.

Passionate about business: a big tick list

Here are just some of the issues that surround us on a day-to-day basis. Tick the ones your organization is going through where you need more buy-in, more passion:

1	Vision of our organization	❑
2	Mission	❑
3	Values	❑
4	Goals	❑
5	Targets	❑
6	Products/services we offer	❑
7	Plans	❑
8	Processes	❑
9	Profits	❑
10	Best practices	❑
11	Customer service	❑
12	New products being launched	❑
13	New services	❑
14	Change programs	❑
15	Total quality	❑
16	Business re-engineering	❑
17	Redundancy/downsizing	❑
18	Merger	❑
19	Acquisition	❑
20	Liquidation	❑
21	Privatization	❑
22	Buy-outs	❑
23	Information technology	❑
24	Balanced scorecard	❑
25	Operational issues	❑
26	Restructuring	❑
27	Marketing issues	❑
28	Sales	❑
29	Human resources	❑
30	Training	❑
31	Development	❑
32	Leadership	❑
33	Career	❑
34	Community issues	❑
35	Union issues	❑
36	Shareholder issues	❑
37	Supplier issues	❑
38	Strategic alliance issues	❑
39	Corporate issues	❑
40	and lots more!	❑

The big question is ... what is your thinking on any or all of these forty issues? Here are the questions to get deep into understanding 'where you are at' and what are you passionate about. This is our ultimate status check, coming up soon.

When it comes to any of the above, such as the Vision or mission of your organization ...

> *We will be No. 1 by the end of this year.*

- **Say** – what do you say about it when you talk to others? e.g. I agree/ disagree/ love it/ hate it.
- **Do** – What do you do about it? e.g. I am working towards it by .../ I am doing absolutely nothing!

> *Kill the competition.*

- **Think** – What do you think about it? e.g. I probably would do it differently but I am giving it my all anyway/I think the person who thought of it has never let us down.
- **Believe** – What do you believe? e.g. I firmly believe that we are going in the right direction/I believe this company is going down the tubes.

> *We are downsizing by 10,000 people.*

- **Feel** – What do you feel about it? e.g. I feel uncomfortable that we are going to try to .../I feel that the others in the organization are not behind all this
- **Results** – What are you doing to affect the top line sales, the costs in the middle and the bottom line profit? e.g. I am working every hour in the day to get to see our customers to get more orders/I am pushing forward this change program to drive out costs to make us the no. 1 in the industry/I am quitting, I hate this place!

These are the questions that will allow us to find out what drives people to do the things they do. More importantly, it will allow us to show others the reasons why they do what they do?

Once you know why people do what they do, then you can start to affect what people do. If they are reacting positively, they may become a role model for Best Practice. If not they are a target for a company to change beliefs and behaviors.

The ultimate STATUS check – on hearts, minds and top and bottom line

WHATEVER it is that people do or say there is more to their behavior than meets the eye. You can find out WHAT and WHY by asking some very basic questions in The Ultimate Status Check. First you ask the question based on the WHAT, WHY and HOW they do what they do, then you ask how do they FEEL when they are doing it. Here is how to do it. Have a note book, and if possible a tape recorder ready. The exact words they say are vital.

Use the T.W.I.S.T.T. graphics to point the way to passion.

- **Doing** – For a STATUS check on the what, how or why people DO the things they do, you point to the pictures in the window on the T.W.I.S.T.T. Are they leaping for joy or the opposite?
- **Saying** – When you are checking what, how and why they SAY the things they say point to the speech bubble. Are they passionate or pissed off?
- **Thinking** – When you research what they THINK, this is the graphic of the 'mind'. Are they thinking YES!!! or NO!!!?
- **Believing** – Researching what they believe, point to the 'heart'. Do they believe in your vision or the opposite?
- **Feeling** – For a STATUS check on how they FEEL about each of these you point to the smiley, or not so smiley faces. Which one are they like, on ANY issue you need to get buy-into?

Point the way to passion

An example of a STATUS check on customer service

Q 'When you are with customers and you are greeting them what do you do?'

A 'I make eye contact by looking up from what I'm doing and smiling. I stop what I'm doing to let them know they have my attention.'

(So far this is pretty classic stuff. The backbone of customer service training films.)

> *I greet every customer like a long lost relative – my mother-in-law!*

Q 'When you are doing this how do you feel? Which one of these faces describes what is going on inside you?'

A 'Do you know, everyone says I look so relaxed but I'm not inside. I find every situation a bit of a challenge. I'm often concerned people will be aggressive or off hand; a lot of people are you know. Really, I'm a bit like the slightly down turned mouth.'

(Now we are really beginning to get into the mind of a sales assistant, and we are beginning to see how we might help them do their job and how we could match their language and concerns, before nudging them to do something extra. Now we're beginning to get some measurable data on their STATUS.)

Q 'What do you say to them?'

A 'That depends. More often than not I'll just say "good morning" or "Hi! I'm here if you need me."'

Q 'What are you feeling at this point?'

A 'I hate pushy sales people myself, so I feel they don't need me jumping on them. I feel good about being there to help but I'm not over the top like that face with the wide grin. Quietly confident, I suppose.'

Q 'What are you thinking?'

A 'I might be thinking, "I remember you from last time, you took ages and didn't buy anything in the end. A bit of a pain in fact!"'

Q 'What are you feeling when you have to serve people who are a "bit of a pain"?'

A 'I feel that it would be nice not to have to deal with the time wasters, but I enjoy this job and problem customers are all part of it.'

(This is good stuff. Most sales assistants will relate to 'problems' often much more readily than 'opportunities'. This is all part of the process of getting to the most important stage of all, beliefs.)

Q 'What do you believe deep down about customer service?'

A 'Do you know, nobody has ever really asked me. They keep showing me videos about how I'm supposed to act but I really believe the job I'm doing is important anyway. I know that I'm not always as helpful as I might be but I love this job, I love meeting new people, I love getting the miserable ones to buy something and feel a bit better themselves.'

Q 'What do you feel about the part you play here?'

A 'It sounds like I'm trying to be a "goody two shoes" but I actually believe this is a good company that looks after its customers, and that is important to me. This is why I work so hard to come across as cheerful, even if I don't feel too good.'

Q 'How does all your work affect things like sales, or keeping our costs under control, and ultimately in our profit?'

A 'I've never really thought about it in those terms. But now you mention it, I like to help people for their sake, not for our departmental figures, or even those awards we get. I do it because I like helping people. I'm now looking after a much larger department than before, so that saves the company money, but even though there used to be two of us I'm getting a bigger monthly total on my own. I like the greater responsibility so I'm throwing my all into it. It make me feel good, knowing I am pulling my weight.'

These questions, digging deep into behavior, are the questions that will allow us to find out what really drives people to do the things they do. Just as importantly, they will allow us to show others IN THEIR OWN WORDS AND LANGUAGE the reasons why their colleagues do what they do.

Good. We have the top performers, what about the rest?

Now you can go and find out the what, why, and how those people who are NOT performing feel. This will allow you to tap into their language and help you 'see' into their hearts and minds.

Once you know WHY people who are not performing do what they do, then you can start to affect WHAT people do.

This is the bottom line to all marketing.

Three key steps take place:

1   where are you now?
2   target the message
3   get a change in beliefs and actions.

Simple really!

Hopefully you are now well and truly hooked into the need to market yourself. Then you will need to really get down to some pretty good targeting of your messages. To do that and to begin really talking the language of marketing, your next move is into the world of your customer. But which ones? Do you treat them all the same? Clearly not. They need to be split into easily understood sections. Some will want this. Others will want that. Some are like this. Others are like that. Some do this. Others do that.

Now is the time to start talking the language of marketing. Now is the time to talk 'market segmentation'. Segmenting your customers into defined groups makes it easier for you to understood them, and to target your messages.

How do marketing people split people into different groups? We have covered in the first five Ss what goes on inside people's heads. In the next chapter we will look at their influences from the outside. The key method of understanding people in marketing is by analyzing and defining two different forces affecting their lives – their social and economic backgrounds.

Now we have a greater understanding of our internal customers. We have a STATUS report on where the 'ideal' stand when it comes to hearts, minds and the passion they feel for what they do. You have done an Ultimate STATUS Check on the best and the 'yet to be best'. You are now ready to get out of people's heads and move into new territory – demographics. First some mental aerobics.

Mental aerobic exercise no. 11:
Don't you get cross with me!

The circles below show the STATUS of the person at work when they are in the mode of Parent, Adult or Child. Write down the type of conversation which goes on when people revert to the STATUS they learned as children.

Does this make for good business? How would you deal with someone who gets mad and waggles their finger at you like a disapproving parent?

 Parent

e.g. You didn't get that report to me. Why the heck not?

 Child

You didn't tell me to!

 Adult

e.g. Are the figures correct?

 Parent

What do you expect? Of course they are!

 Child

e.g. I'm so fed up of it here.

 Adult

Let's meet next week to discuss it formally.

Mental aerobic exercise no. 12:
Just who do you think you are?

Our conversations at work sometimes get tainted by people using their STATUS to influence what happens – and it's not always
the boss! Write down typical examples you have come across.
Once you can spot these situations you'll be better able to deal
with them. The approach people take may be a legacy of the old
'order and obey' days. They may just be 'bossy' people! And the
reactions may be the old stereotypical ones too, when what the
situation calls for is everyone working together.

What do the people below say and do that reflects their STATUS
at work?

Boss ⟵⟶ **Staff**

e.g. If I don't get what I want   Of course I will do it
by next Thursday ...   (by next Friday)

Worker ⟵⟶ **Supervisor**

Union representative ⟵⟶ **Plant manager**

Chief executive ⟵⟶ **Marketing director**

Mental aerobic exercise no. 13:
The ultimate STATUS check –
where do you stand on any issue?

'I'd like to ask you a few questions so I can really understand what you do, say , think and feel about ... e.g. greeting customers.'

If people are doing and saying things that particularly affect the top or bottom line it becomes 'best practice'. If not, you'll find out what behavior needs to change and why.

   What do you **do** when you ...?

   What do you **feel** when you ...?

   What do you **think** when you ...?

   What do you **believe** when you ...?

   What affect does it have on the **top line** (sales/ customer relations) or **bottom line** (profit)?

SOCIAL – THE SIXTH S OF SUCCESS

How does your background affect how you think?

We are the sum of our experiences – and some have had more experiences than others, but how do we know what to look for?

Find out how the science of marketing applies as much to researching and targeting your internal customers as it does to your external customers.

*W*hat is this chapter about?

This chapter shows you the external influences that result in how people think and behave.

*H*ow you benefit

This knowledge will allow you to get really close to your internal customers and create a map of the external influences on the personality, the culture of individuals and of whole organizations.

*Y*ou will gain most by ...

... learning how to think like a marketeer. Psychographics, demographics, target markets, targeting; all of these add up to knowing how to create committed customers that buy into your products and services. The rules can be applied to all your relationships.

SOCIAL – the forces shaping human nature

Relationship marketing

Relationship marketing is all about developing strong relationships with your customers – becoming 'best friends', for life if you can.

Now here comes the crunch.

If you are going to create a lifetime relationship with someone it is important to know who it is you are making friends with.

Up until now it may not have been necessary for the marketing profession to even consider some of the more esoteric concepts of psychology. There was even less need for marketing to be associating itself with any 'New Age' concepts of behavior. It was definitely not a good idea to be seen to be considering some of the quirky 'alternative' approaches, or cultural, or ethnic approaches to studying human behavior. What might marketing have to do with Zen, for example, or Yin and Yang? Marketing was having enough of a struggle with its own image. In one motor manufacturing organization I know, the marketing department are called the 'flower arrangers'!

Not until now has there been the need to spare a thought for the inner worlds of things like geometric psychology, color psychology, gender psychology, Neuro Linguistic Programming. We've looked at them and seen how powerful they are. Now let's turn to the outer world that has been the traditional domain of marketing. Let's see if it can be applied to create passion at work.

Demographics – the maps of people territory

'Demography is the study of human populations in terms of size, density, location, age, sex, race, occupation and other statistics. The demographic environment is of major interest to marketers because it involves people, and people make up markets.' (Professor Philip Kotler, *Principles of Marketing*.)

If you turn to the T.W.I.S.T.T. (p. 19) and look at the windows under **Social** you will see the pictures that represent the external influences on our lives. Unlike the psychographics (lifestyle measurements), which we have covered under the first five Ss, these influences stem more from WHERE we are rather than WHO we are.

Put simply, if you're a 23-year-old male native of Borneo, living in a tribal village in the jungle, you will think, speak, act and do things in a completely different way to a 96-year-old lady residing in an expensive old people's retirement home by the seaside in southern California.

A 96-year-old will want different things to a 23-year-old. A male will want different things to a female. A southern Californian will want different things to someone from Borneo. Someone in the jungle will want different things to a dweller in a retirement home. A person with little income will want different things to a person with a large income. There's a picture already emerging from this small amount of data. All without adding on the many other social and economic or psychological influences.

Each of the social, and economic, influences can have a huge bearing on understanding people. But what you may ask has this got to do with your relationships at work? In the past maybe not much. As long as they understood you then you treated them as 'employees' who did what they were told. Now times have changed – a lot. Until the last four decades, even in the west, people have lived in small communities without the benefits of personal means of transport, telephones and television. Now people have access to cheap global travel, technology and three dimensional entertainment. These consumers at home are employees at work. And they don't like being 'told' what to do by anybody. The way to their hearts and minds inside work is now to appeal to them as your customers. This requires a new approach.

How? By understanding people so well that you know exactly what they will respond to. How do you do that? The psychographics, covered in the first five Ss, gets you into the hearts and minds of people's inner worlds. Demographics helps you get an understanding of people's outer worlds. This comes from asking some basic questions. The sophisticated bit comes from interpreting the data.

Where do you/did you live?

The map of the USA in the window on the T.W.I.S.T.T indicates the first part of the jigsaw – your geographic influences. Pointing to a map gives rise to a simple question and often a simple answer.

Q   Where do you/did you live?
A   Los Angeles.

When it comes to people at work, geography will matter. The people at Head Office in a down town office location will have completely different views to the factory worker based in the industrial belt, or the technology worker based at home. How do you reach all three? With different messages? The answer is increasingly a very big YES.

As we move more into a multicultural and global society with tremendous mobility of work forces it will become increasingly important to find what geographic influences people have, in both their background and their current location.

The geographic influences are many and varied, and too great to cover here. My intention is to bring the awareness of this external factor to the foreground. Recruitment advertising, or communicating internally during a company's relocation from one site to another often places great emphasis on the geographic influences (like the quality of life and schools). Once installed, however, the external influences tend to be ignored. Yet a community can have a great deal of influence over the people in it. This is one of the reasons why an integrated approach to dealing with people is beginning to be realized as a vital component of a total approach to all an organization's stakeholders.

Community relations are no longer just 'exercises', they are an on-going program.

"Don't you dump your waste in my back garden – the rest of the world."

What is interesting is how global organizations are now operating global community relations programs. The Coca Cola (on-going) sponsorship of the 1996 Atlanta Olympic Games is a good example. Businesses are reaching out to the community. People grow up and live in communities. This is where they get their influences.

Businesses, communities and the people who live and work in them are beginning to understand each other, and work together a lot more. Let's face it, businesses ARE part of the community.

Once all these inter-related influences are understood as part of the overall mix in marketing to internal customers, then getting through to the hearts and minds of the people who live and work in their communities will be a lot easier.

What sort of house do you live in?

Over the last quarter of a century a very sophisticated form of map making has arisen, based on the type of house you live in. In the UK the most significant form of this sprang out of the 1971 Population Census, which not only covered who lived where, but a range of topics including the type of dwelling they lived in.

> *We're a two kids, two cats, two cars, two house family.*

Research companies were then able to classify people according to their residential neighborhood type and use it in marketing. It is not hard to predict that people in a farming community are likely to have Land Rover, Jeep or Volvo and a Labrador dog. By conducting further research they found those people may prefer to buy Australian wine and holiday in the Bahamas, very different to someone living in a one-bedroom rented high rise in an inner city area.

Once you know that people in a certain type of dwelling will purchase certain types of products you can target your direct mail accordingly. Have you ever wondered how companies decide to send you things in the post?

Your address is giving away more about you than you ever imagined!

Basically, your house defines your lifestyle and indicates your consumer preference. Your lifestyle will also show up in the way you act at work. You may prefer to move and work with others with this lifestyle. You may also be highly motivated to keep this lifestyle.

Home is where the heart (and mind) is

A 45-year-old executive with a six-bedroom house in the country with a swimming pool, may work considerably longer hours than a 20-year-old living in a flat with friends in town, who goes frequently to clubs.

Different lifestyles at work have far-reaching implications for getting to others' hearts and minds. If your lifestyle creates the motivators to work then finding out about lifestyle will get you closer to what creates the passion you need in business.

Knowing where people are from is all part of knowing 'where they are coming from'. The way to find out is to ask them. The more feedback you have, the better your targeting will be, as long as you are using the right data.

The way you can begin to collect that data is through the **T.W.I.S.T.T. Success Generator**. For each of the components on social and economic data as well as the other Six Ss, you can use this information to target your message.

Now let's look at some more data which will help you to target and get buy-in to your message.

How old are you?

> *It took me 40 years to get to the top and 40 minutes to be shown the door.*

This is a question which is beginning to attract its own band of devotees, especially if you're over 40. The older you are, it appears, the less chance you have of getting a job. 'Early retirement' has become a euphemism for redundancy. 'Redundancy' has become a euphemism for 'You're fired'.

For some reason the implication seems to be that 'You can't teach an old dog new tricks'. Yet looking at the psychographics we have covered in the Six Ss, does age really matter? My father, a Squiggle, is still inventing things, and coming up with new ideas well past his retirement. If you let a Squiggle loose on just about anything, they will probably come up with a better way – no matter how old they are. And if you show a Box something that is tried and tested, or requires their input in making it tried and tested, then they are just as likely to help – with a great deal of enthusiasm. Of course many people don't like change, it is uncomfortable. But who decided change is an ageist issue?

The sad thing is, by getting rid of older people an organization's KNOWLEDGE is being lost, not just its people.

A person's age has a huge bearing on their attitudes, beliefs and desires. As organizations segment their external audiences to even more sophisticated levels, this will have an effect on how they communicate to people internally, so they can relate to people who may or may not be like them.

Can a 23-year-old female telemarketing operator really understand the needs of a 65-year-old male, retired chief executive?

So you can see that the new skill of the 21st century will not be customer service, as in 'How can I help you?', it will be the marketing skills of understanding and targeting customers, in order to build lifetime relationships.

Yes, I'm the customer services director – so is everyone else here.

On top of our actual job we will all be marketing managers of ourselves, and our company. We will not only be the public face of the brand names we represent, we will be the brand managers responsible for our bit of the brand that the customer sees – us.

Our job will be as Brand Ambassadors, representing our brands externally, and as Brand Managers we will be able to take what we learn and apply our knowledge internally.

Now that I have just promoted you, bear this in mind as we come to the next section.

What job do you do?

Are you a manager, techno-wizard, car mechanic or washroom atten-dant? Whatever you are, you may have some messages that you want to communicate to get others to do things differently. The question is, who are you targeting your messages to?

Are you targeting your messages upwards to more 'senior' people. This may be important if they are likely to have a strong influence on what you want or believe. Getting your message right may be vital, to you, to them, to everyone else. Are they a Triangle? If they are, then messages about profit, costs and results will be appreci-ated. The more senior they are the less time they may have, so a short, sharp message may also be vital. How many long boring re-ports with all the arguments laid out in great detail do you think they are likely to read? What job do they do? If it is marketing they will want to hear marketing speak. If they are accountants then throw them the numbers. If they are IT specialists then get technical. And so it goes on.

Are you targeting your colleagues of equal status? If they are in a different job to you do you really think they are interested in your problems?

Are you targeting people 'down the line'? Now is the time to avoid being patronizing. Targeting down the line does not mean talking down to someone.

Your target customer may be young, inexperienced, naive or older, experienced and fed up with all the initiatives the organization keeps throwing at them. Whatever they are, it is their job, not yours that is the most important thing to them.

The latest vision, mission and values may not matter one jot to people if they don't know where they will be sitting in the next reshuffle.

If sitting next to Mary is important, then answering this need is crucial. If they feel that they are hindered from doing a good job for whatever reason, then they won't be interested in the reasons for something unrelated to them.

Does this sound like common sense? If it is then why is it that in a recent study the following commonly happens?

Of all the messages that staff wanted to hear, the typical business media (like the company magazine and notice board) only covered 7% of top issues they felt pertinent to them.

What people do is so important to them that they want to hear about THEIR issues first. Conversely, everyone seems to think that what is important to them must be important to everyone else. So here we have the great communication paradox.

In all walks of life people want to talk about THEIR issues. But if no-one wants to hear about your problems or your opportunities because they are only interested in theirs, then we have a problem!

Everyone needs to figure out that you have to start listening to other people's problems and opportunities first, if you want them to listen to yours. The route to doing this is called LISTENING. The marketing term is called RESEARCH. They are the same thing.

So, from a marketing and targeting point of view, research is vital. If you are looking to get your message across, then knowing what information people need to do their job is vital. It is only by getting information through to people that they can learn, develop, grow and increase their knowledge and skills. Recent studies show that like Uranium, which is only half as active in a set time, so people's skills now have a half life as well. Learning is now critical – to everyone.

Above the line – below the line (marketing speak)
Down the line – up the line (management speak)

"
Let's talk about me for a change.
"

How long will it be before you are using only half of the knowledge that you are using today? The latest indications are that your skills 'half life' will come within three years.

What has this got to do with targeting messages to people? Once the importance of constantly updating your skills is realized then learning will be one of the biggest motivators (or 'hooks') you will find. Once people recognize that their job will only be safe if they keep up with the way learning needs to be done, then something amazing will happen. Once people finally understand that their job will be overtaken by the need to do something completely different, then a new marketing approach will occur.

If I knew then half as much as I know now I'd be twice as informed – I think.

Instead of companies relying on a top-down 'push strategy' for communication, they will ALSO be able to rely on people developing their own 'pull strategy'. Instead of people being force fed information, being sent on a training course, having to sit and watch a boring video, grudgingly going to a team briefing, watching flashing screen savers they are not interested in, the reverse will apply.

The new yearn to learn – the ultimate 'pull strategy'

- People will seek out information.
- People will be passionate about finding out what is going on.
- People will realize that learning will be part of their survival kit.
- Tools like the Internet and the Intranet will become *'must haves'*, both from a company point of view and an individual's.

It will be a person's job that will dictate what information they need. This will create a 'pull' for information that will come from the customer, the stakeholders or supplier. For example, the ability to screen out certain information that arrives in your e-mail means that it is the customer who is becoming the 'gate-keeper', not the organization.

In the past, the way people got their information was almost by spoon feeding them. The organization trained you and developed you to do what it wanted you to do. You were given instructions, you had 'on the job training', you went on training courses, you may have been sponsored for academic courses. You had briefings from your manager, got a copy of the company newspaper and went to the occasional road-show.

Times have changed. The organization cannot spoon feed you any more. The new technology of the Internet and Intranet is there for a different purpose. Now it is truly a 'pull strategy'. It is you who is responsible for accessing the data that you need to do your job now and in the future.

Life is just too complicated to take it 'nice and easy', and map out a long-term training and development plan for yourself. Learning is now a constant exercise. Developing yourself is a lifetime need.

The implications for accessing the information you need are enormous. Now it is an organization's knowledge and its communication that will determine its success. The same is true for you.

So how do you contribute to this in your job? First of all, you contribute to an organization's knowledge with what you ADD to the organization. It is up to you to increase the information base of your organization. This is one of the reasons you are there, it is called 'adding value'. Second you contribute with what you TAKE OUT and how you USE the information you access.

Pull (not push) button technology

"
*Tell me what you
want what you
really really want.*
"
Marketing Spice

Your job will rely on being able to input and to access information. When you input information, people must WANT to read and use what you input, otherwise why bother? Targeted information will be crucial. When you access information, it must also be targeted to you so that you WANT to read it and use it to the benefit of the organization.

Inputting data alone will no longer be sufficient in the hope that someone will use it or stumble on it. Entering information alone will no longer be sufficient, if the information does little more than inform.

- Targeted information that creates buy-in and action will be vital.
- We already have too much data and information – what we want is knowledge ('applied information) and behavioral change.
- The key to success will be to have information that people want and use.

It won't just be the internal information that will be crucial. The information from ALL the external stakeholders is just as vital as well. What are your customers trying to achieve? What is the job they are having to do?

Getting close to them and their needs is what all these 'Total Quality' type programs were all about. Yet where in all these programs did you learn about their hearts and minds?

The old saying goes 'the way to a man's heart is through his stomach'; in other words, you get to people through their needs. What this means is that the way to a person's heart is through helping them achieve what THEY want. In part this may be to do a *better job*, i.e. *faster, quicker, cheaper*. This is where working out all those Quality problems may benefit them. It is just as likely that what they want will come from all the other forces that drive them. For example, the Squiggles will have fun coming up with new ways of improving things. The Triangles will be happy if it makes more profit. The Circles may just enjoy the team spirit of working on the problem together.

A focus on the technical aspects of improving the quality, speed and cost of what you do may be important. People understand this in their heads.

A focus on the emotional issues of having fun, creating things, buttoning down detail will appeal to their hearts. Passion lies in capturing and mobilizing the head *and* the heart.

Doing the job alone is no longer doing your job. Pleasing yourself, your customers and suppliers will dictate your success and theirs. And if you do a good job, how much will you earn?

How much do I get paid?

Pay is an emotive issue. It may seem to be high on people's list of needs yet all too often our research shows that it is often not a motivator at all.

> "I'm overpaid and underworked. Or is it the other way round?"

How much we are paid does affect what we buy, where we live, who we socialize with, and where we socialize with them. Do we meet at the local soup kitchen or at the opera?

People at either end of the economic scale are turned on or off by completely different things. More than that, they speak in completely different ways, using very different words and style.

This brings me neatly to how the language you speak influences the hearts and minds of others.

What language do you speak?

As every country becomes more and more multi-racial, and multi-languaged, the forms of language twist and turn every second of the day. The implication is that if you want to get through to a 22-year-old New Yorker, born and bred 'on the street', you will best do it in their language, or at least understand where they are coming from. The same is true for a London stockbroker or a Japanese worker.

Language is becoming a real issue as we become not just international in business, but truly global. It doesn't stop with the multitude of mother tongues. Business language is forming and evolving as we speak. Technical languages are becoming more pervasive. If you aren't 'surfing the Web', and trying to impress your colleagues at work with the latest techno-speak, then you're nobody!

How do you get through to others in this multi-languaged, multi-layered, multi-disciplined, multi-faceted world of ours.

The answer is no longer as simple as learning to speak another language.

Translating is not targeting.

This message is worth repeating as it is a core message in this new global village of ours.

Translating is not targeting.

Translating is not targeting.

Translating is not targeting.

Translating is not targeting.

Translating is not targeting.

Even in our own tongue, what is heard is NOT what we say. What is heard is affected by all the psychographic and demographic factors we have covered so far.

And there is more! What we hear and what we say is made even more complicated by these other social influences on us.

What is your religion or creed?

Now we're starting to go really deep. From a 'beliefs' point of view this is the window into the heart. Be it religion or values, what people hold deep inside them is the key to their anger or their love, their pride and their passion.

> We are doing this in the name of
> ....
> (fill in blank).

It is the strength of the positive and negative forces of our beliefs that drive us as human beings and bring out our passion.

Capturing hearts and minds is about tapping into beliefs.

People bring their beliefs, their religion and creed to work with them. They also bring their values about society, work and how to treat their fellow citizens and colleagues.

How do beliefs affect the way we do business?

Passion at work – the holy grail

We bolt our own business creeds on to the beliefs people already bring with them. We try to change, mould, adapt, alter, instill and release what we in business think the business needs.

If your organization hasn't got a mission, vision and values (although you may not call them these names) then you are almost alone.

Visions, missions and values are the route to instill an almost religious set of goals and principles into the people of an organization.

Why is this?

- To mobilize hearts and minds.
- To generate the passion that releases energy and enthusiasm.
- To deliver better business results that come from the drive to adopting best practices and innovating new ideas.

There is a huge well of untapped passion just waiting to be tapped inside every individual.

If only we knew how to get to it.

Just look at the way people throw themselves into projects and hobbies at home. What could organizations do with this tremendous resource? A lot!

It is here that we can go back to a discipline like Neuro Linguistic Programming, which helps people to understand and articulate their beliefs and release their untapped passion and energy.

The passion is already inside us.

An organization's vision, mission and values may help us all move in the same direction. Wouldn't it be better if we could ADD these to an already motivated and passionate workforce?

The skills and tools that release passion can come from marketing. This is the power of this discipline. But first we need to go deeper still.

Where do we get our particular religion or creed? Mostly we got them from where we grew up, and in what ethnic background we were raised.

What is your ethnic origin?

Just as language is having a massive impact on the globalization of business, so too is the effect of ethnic background. Surviving in a multicultural world is 'do or die' stuff. The message? Understand culture or else!

Until recently, the assumption at work seems to have been that even with this incredible cultural mix all around us we have a 'mass market'.

The internal mass market

- In work we don't have cultural diversity we have a mass market called 'employees'.
- Or are they a homogeneous lot we call staff?
- If we don't like this title we call them 'associates'.
- Or if we think we should treat them as equals we call them 'partners'.

If only the single word we use made us realize that they are all totally different.

The word to describe the people we are trying to satisfy externally is not a mass market. They are called CUSTOMERS.

As soon as we say 'customers' we know it means so much more than 'people who buy your products or services'.

" Just put me through to someone who can help me. You are the seventh 'relationship manager' I've talked to! "

We now have a whole discipline trying to get through to customers, which we call marketing. We have another disciple trying to entice them to part with their money called sales, and another trying to keep them happy called customer service.

If organizations are to succeed, then with such marginal differences between them and their competitors, it is the people that will make the difference. In global organizations these people will come from a multi-cultural melting pot. And each one will have to be treated differently.

The real issue will be capturing the hearts and minds of everyone in your multi-cultural world – both inside and outside the organization.

What is your family size?

" Everyone I meet I'm related to these days. "

What is your family size, or more to the point, what is your family made up of? How many stepfathers, mothers, children, brothers, sisters, uncles, aunts, half brothers, sisters, live-in relations and non-relations, foster parents, and so on, are in your family?

Divorce in the West is rife. Why? We go back to what was said at the beginning of the book. Communication – lack of it, or the wrong kind of it is a huge factor in the break up of families. Almost every one of us is personally affected. If people could communicate and be capable of talking through all those issues that drive them apart wouldn't this be a better world? If people could retain the love, respect, dignity and harmony that we all crave then the massive changes we face in society would not be such a destructive force on our family life.

The point is, our home life does not stay at home. We bring all our 'baggage' to work with us, our trials and tribulations, our worries about our relationships as well as our futures. How are we supposed to feel passionate when in fact we feel desperate?

We all have needs, motivations and desires that we look to be fulfilled at home. Successful families learn to meet those needs. The same can be true at work.

Organizations have a direct route to the hearts and minds of the people who work in them.

They provide the companionship, the teams, the stimulation the challenges, the fun, the friends and, in a lot of cases, the partners in the home! Yet it is here that the conflict occurs.

Outsourcing, hot desking and virtual teams doesn't sound too much like close business relationships, team building and having a great time out with the people at work.

Charles Handy in his book *The Empty Raincoat* talks of the crazy situation where cutting out jobs creates a jobless society for those who are desperate to work, and a stressed out 70-hour week for those who are desperate to be at home. This is the net result of our search for efficiency. We have created an 'empty raincoat' that hangs uselessly on the peg when everyone is being 'rained on' (my words) from a great height.

Home (working) sweet home (working)

It is difficult to get passionate about anything if you are desperately trying to feed your family, or have difficult relationships with them because you are never there.

Why are we talking about family life here, in a book about business?

As employers, colleagues, team leaders or team members, if we want to tap into people's hearts and minds and release this thing called passion we need to understand what motivates people. We don't have to pry, just understand. We can act as marketeers who understand their customers so well they are able to satisfy their very specific needs, wants and desires.

We're all just one happy family at work.

So there it is. The last of the social influences. It is now time to move on to the most important bit – how to turn this 'information' into 'knowledge'.

It is time to start to move into the second phase of marketing – how to:

- target your message so that you can mobilize hearts and minds
- tap into the passion that exists already
- affect the business results by changing the actions and behaviors of the people in your organization.

Before that here is your last set of mental aerobics.

Mental aerobic exercise no. 14:
Just where are you coming from?

Any person's background will be very different to anyone else you talk to. In the 'old days', everyone was brought up in the same village. Now the world is a huge melting pot. Just listen to the story of their life. Listen to the words they use as you talk to them about their social and economic backgrounds. The more data you gather, the easier it will be to find out just where they are coming from.

Tell me about it ...

Name _____   Date _____

Your national influences Which region or country have you lived in? Do you have any strong affiliations? e.g. a Jamaican Rastafarian with a strong affiliation to Ethiopia; an Irish American with a strong affiliation to Sinn Fein; a Norwegian expatriate who has lived abroad for 20 years with no sense of 'roots'.

Your local influences What sort of house? What sort of neighborhoods have you lived in, or live in now? How does this affect your life?

How old are you? What influences have affected you as you have got older? e.g. a child of the 30s, 40s, 50s, 60s, 70s, etc., wars, slumps, booms, cultural swings, from Yuppies to the Great Depression.

Tell me more about it ...

What industry are you in? What are the culture and people like where you work? What job do you do? Do you like it? Are you looking to change? What education did you have to get the job? What is it like where you work?

How much do you earn? What income do you earn and spend? What sort of lifestyle do you have?

What language(s) do you speak and with what sort of accent? How has your language or ability to speak languages helped?

What religious beliefs do you hold? These will dictate some of your strongest personal values.

What ethnic influences do you have?, e.g. Eskimo, Arab, New Yorker, Spanish, Rastafarian, British.

What is your family size and diversity? Are you married, single, partnered, divorced, gay, widowed? Do you have children, an extended family?

PART 3

THE PASSION PACK

The 'How To' Mobilize Hearts and Minds, and Generate Buy-In to Change

Section 3

What is this section about?

This section gives you the practical tools to get on with the job of capturing and mobilizing hearts and minds. I have called it 'The Passion Pack' to arouse your desire! It gives you tried and tested methods for (1) researching your customers – Watch; (2) using the language they use – Match; (3) targeting your message – Nudge; and (4) getting feedback on the results – Buy-in.

How you benefit

On a practical level you get easy to use tools that deliver results. You get simple ways to achieve quick wins and long-term success.

You will gain most by ...

... imagining you are creating the best ever marketing campaign; acting as though you are the world's best research agency; thinking you are the world's greatest advertising genius when writing your copy and designing your piece of communication.

A target is something you aim at

One of the best examples of a target is the one used in archery. It's colorful, easy to recognize and gives you feedback on how well you have done. The lowest scores are on the outside the highest in the middle – the bullseye! We will use the analogy of this archery target. Remember people as targets don't stand still, they move, constantly!

In this section you will learn how to aim your arrows at a moving target, one that is constantly changing shape as well. Once you know the nature of your target you can learn to hit the bullseye every time. The rings of the target will depict the principles of Watch, Match and Nudge. What is at the centre? **Hearts and minds and buy-in.**

Watch – the T.W.I.S.T.T. Success Generator

On the outer ring of the target are the six Ss of Success you have already covered. This 'How To' section is the T.W.I.S.T.T. Success Generator, which we met at the beginning, to record your data. Boxes will love it. Squiggles will have to learn to love it!

Match – the 'one liners reminders'

The next inner ring on our target is for matching what you say with your customer. It contains a reminder of the types of words, phrases, language patterns and the 'one liners' that people use – so you can as well.

Nudge – the 'WHY Communicate Framework'

And now comes the part that helps you learn to hit the bullseye – how to put your message across when you want to 'Nudge' others forward. The WHY Communicate Framework is the surefire way to express yourself so that you move them in towards buy-in.

Buy-in – the 'SWOTcheck™' on hearts and minds

Only others can give you their hearts and minds. But how do you know if you have them? Have you captured their imagination and their feelings? Do you know what's good about what you are trying to get across? Do you know what could be better? What new ideas do they have? What would stop them from giving you their future commitment? SWOTcheck™ is the research tool anyone can use. Its structure of **S**trengths, **W**eaknesses, **O**pportunities and **T**hreats provides you with a tool for getting feedback from others and helping you plan what to do with it.

N.B. SWOTcheck™ is a registered trademark. If you are interested, my company The Marketing and Communication Agency is developing a software version, easy to use and providing instant results for better targeting. (End of advert!)

Watch, Match and Nudge – the 'how to' of all time

Bullseye

> *Don't believe a word they say.*

You have encountered the concept of watch, match and nudge in the sections on SEX and SENSES, under the topic of creating 'rapport'.

Throughout this book the quotes by the side of the main text are an illustration of the principle of Watch, Match and Nudge. Look at these quotes carefully now that you understand the six *S*s. They are

EXACTLY the sort of things that people say as we take them through the thinking behind Passion at Work. They are the sort of thing YOU might say. There are Squiggle quotes, Box quotes, Yellow quotes and a few 'Black' ones too. There are Female and Male quotes, and quotes using visual, auditory and kinaesthetic language. Why bother putting then in? Consider these questions.

- Did you read the quotes by the side of the text in the book?
- Did you relate to them?
- Did they sound like YOU might have said them?
- Were some of them sceptical?
- Were some them challenging?
- Did some sound as though they came from real people saying real things?
- Did you leaf through the book and feel comfortable about reading things in quotes that others might have said?
- Did it reassure you that the different views expressed showed the book did not contain a one-sided view?
- Did it appear that someone had actually LISTENED to a variety of opinions and was happy to have other views expressed?

> *I've been misquoted again.*

If, having thought through these questions you came to two fundamental conclusions, then you have grasped the power of the first two parts of Watch and Match.

Watch People like to be listened to

Match People relate to things they (not you) are already thinking or saying.

The trouble is that the way people communicate in business (and out of it) is the exact opposite of Watch and Match!

Don't watch I love people to listen to me

Don't match I love the sound of my own voice, and to hear myself expressing my own dearly held thoughts, ideas and beliefs.

As a principle Watch and Match is the simplest of things to apply. You can do it on just about any aspect of communication. The principle is easy.

They say it – you say it or play it back.

No, not parrot fashion! Although you can do that with quotes in text. You repeat things back in a way that the other person KNOWS you have listened. The 'how to' is shown below.

You can also play back 'exactly' what was said in the content of any media that allows sound. Good old fashioned 'vox pops', the voice of the people will persuade anyone that you have at least listened. You may not do anything about it, but you have at least listened. This is the most crucial step in marketing.

What is it that you are playing back? Try this for a list.

MATCH – the things to play back

- words
- phrases
- sentences
- feelings
- ideas
- flights of fancy
- figures

- concerns
- problems
- one-liners
- solutions
- fears
- opinions
- facts

Whatever anyone says, if they think it worth saying then it will benefit you to acknowledge what they are saying and play it back. Not all the time, but enough to show you care.

How do you do it? The easiest word of all to remember to use when you want to reflect back what someone has just said is 'so …'. This little word will help you more than any other when it comes to gaining rapport, and playing back what people say.

Play back with 'so ...'

'So what you are saying is that ...'
'So you think that if the competition do that it will ...'
'So this is what you think you should do next?'
'So you did this when he did that?'
'So you felt bad when Mary said that?'
'So you believe that if I went ahead with this it will succeed?'

Watch and Match on written communication

Written communication is very different to verbal communication. The live action and immediate feedback using a technique like 'So ...' is missing. The trick is to put back the feedback from your target audience into your copy. This of course assumes that you have gone out and gathered the feedback first.

What if something is urgent or secret?

If something is that urgent or secret that you can't Watch and Match then go ahead, and don't expect to get buy-in! You might, if you have built lots of rapport. Remember this:

64% of people don't believe senior managers.

Surely it is better to test even those things which are top secret. Tom Peters calls them 'chicken tests' after the failure of Rolls Royce to do some quick tests on a new light weight carbon fibre aircraft engine. After many years of work and a mammoth and multi-million pound investment program, the new engines were finally tested to see if

" Are you calling me a liar? "

So, so, quick quick so

they would cope with a bird flying into the engines. The first (dead) chicken thrown into the new engine made the carbon fibre propeller explode into tiny pieces. If only they had 'chicken tested' a mock up prototype in the first few weeks!

'Chicken testing' is another word for research. How many failures on take off have you seen on the launch of visions, missions, values, new products, services, change programs? You must surely be able to find someone you trust with your 'secret'.

Having done your research through verbal communication, and when you have your quotes about what others think, here is where copy writing comes in.

You can now write the vox pops statements that create rapport.

- A number of you have said 'Actual quote'

OR

- A number of you have said that …
- I have heard a few people say '…'
- Peter Jones in a recent document said '…'
- 'We don't believe you'. This has been stated by many of you in a recent survey
- 'Give us the facts' is a cry that many people have uttered since the talks about a merger started.

> *Vision cluck cluck*
> *Mission cluck cluck*
> *Values cluck cluck*
> *Goals cluck cluck*
> *Anything cluck cluck*
>
> A chicken testing

> *Our readership is up to 94% (from only 33%) with this new journal. Well done!*
>
> A client of ours

Compare these quotes to the 'sound of my own voice' type of copy.

- I have been saying for some time that …
- I want you all to know that …
- My recent document of 15th June stated that …
- We are very concerned about the lack of trust in the company so we have decided to …
- Here are the facts. The merger between us and XYZ is not going to happen.

> *Blah, blah, blah, blah, blah, blah, blah, blah, blah, blah, blah, blah, blah, blah, blah*

Which did you relate to? Which were you inclined to believe? On the next pages are a selection of Watch and Match real quotes from a large variety of Business Journals my company produces for many well-known international organizations.

Real people saying real things in real companies going through real change

How did we get the quotes? Through good old market research. We went out and we talked with people. We used our internal marketing model. You will see quotes about issues from pay to corporate strategy. Once people see that you can 'match' their concerns then you can move forward – and only then.

'I need to be listened to about the daily business things and I need feedback.'

'How is the firm improving its image?'

'Tell the staff when they are doing things well.'

'WISH IT HAD HAPPENED EARLIER.'

'Pay for performance — if you claim to do it, do it.'

'We know the acronyms but we don't know what they mean.'

'If the client care survey is not acted on, the vision will not be achieved.'

'What's in it for me?'

'The booklet and the meeting were a good combination.'

'Do we differ fundamentally from the competition?'

'A good discussion, but will anything happen?'

'We need a central communication point.'

'It is too complicated. Why don't we have some simple things that everyone understands?'

'We have to take a longer view about market share.'

'We will require total commitment from the top to make this work.'

'We need to pull together as one company — I don't think we do now.'

'What about job security?'

'Isn't this just another way of keeping pay rises down?'

'I would like to know who wants my opinion.'

'What do our competitors pay? I haven't got a clue.'

'Where do we see the industry in 5–10 years' time?'

'I really don't understand what it's about.'

'There's almost no cascade of information down the management chain (or upwards either!)'

'Locally I'm listened to, but beyond my boss not much happens.'

'We are not a well known brand. We need to raise our profile.'

'If the chiefs don't fight then the Indians won't fight.'

'THERE MUST BE TRUST BETWEEN MANAGEMENT AND STAFF.'

'If we improve on what we are doing, know what we are aiming for and pull together in a united company, anything can be achieved.'

'We don't know what's going on in other units. There should be more liaison.'

'But when I look at the job ads in the paper, it looks like I'm very underpaid.'

'At the end of the day we have to satisfy our shareholders.'

'What are the plans for the future? Will we be growing or shrinking the company?'

'There's no real clarity of why we are doing what we are doing.'

'We must organise ourselves better to react to our customers' needs.'

'I have felt that my work is valued by my department, but I'm not sure it is globally.'

'The whole organisation needs to share the same values and attitudes to the customer.'

'WHERE DO WE SIT IN THE WHOLE SCHEME OF THINGS?'

'I would be more confident in our success if I knew what the objectives were and how I could participate in achieving them.'

'We need to make managers understand the overall goals and then pass on clear objectives to employees.'

The internal marketing model to changing behavior

Here again are the three simple steps to buy-in.

Watch   By getting information – including as many quotes as you can get.

Match   By using their quotes and language and finding the 'hooks' people want.

Nudge   By exciting them with your ideas which can often as not have come from them as well!

Three hints and tips when you do your research

If you did your research well, then you will have asked three things:

1   What is their profile, or what are their six Ss? – so you can understand their motivators. (You can either directly ask them for their Six S profile or guess from the words they use.)
2   What words/language are they using? – so you can play it back to them.
3   What were their hooks? – so you can match their needs to the needs of your business.

Watch – the T.W.I.S.T.T. Success Generator

What you need to start you off on the outer ring of your target, is not a complicated data bank of everyone's type. In keeping with our KISS principle it is the basics that will help you. You can always get more sophisticated as you go along.

The T.W.I.S.T.T. Success Generator is a kind of ready reckoner. It is set out for you to build a basic profile of the individuals you deal with. It is also there to highlight the similarities and the differences between the people that you deal with in teams. By having a list of people's types, especially if they work in teams, you will soon spot the reasons why some people and their teams work well, and why some don't. To take an obvious example, imagine a single Squiggle shut up in a room full of Boxes! This is why Belbin when he describes his team type refers to the Squiggle as a 'Plant'. This refers to the fact that you only leave them 'planted' for a very short time – otherwise everyone gets edgy.

A word of warning

> "
> I know you are all
> dying to hear what I
> have to say.
> "

Clearly the whole purpose of learning the profiles and types of your colleagues and team members is to be able to target them with your messages, but don't think this is going to overwhelm your own individual approach to things. Let's face it, you are who you are.

- Whilst you can think through the important messages you need to target, and you can modify your approach to your audience, you don't want to lose the spirit or essence of you.
- Your words are important in generating passion.
- People want to hear from you, once they know you have listened to them.

Segmenting your message

Equally as important as targeting messages to individuals or people in a team situation is segmenting what you want them to do. For example:

Don't expect the Squiggles to do a very good job on Boxy detail.

Once you know that you have a Squiggle, Box, Triangle or Circle in your team you can get them to work on what they are good at. This is the basis of team building. Pretty much all the various definitions of team types will be the same as the ones defined in the six *S*s. However, this book is about targeting, not team building. So here is the Success Generator for team type targeting.

How do you use it?

Simple:

1   Ask the questions in the Success Generator
2   Fill out the responses in the blank spaces
3   Use the information to target your messages.

We have put this longer version of the T.W.I.S.T.T. Success Generator you met at the beginning to allow you to fill it out on a real person. Remember, though, this material is copyright – thanks!

The T.W.I.S.T.T. Success Generator

Name _____ Date _____

Your influences: What you say, do, think and feel:

Shapes

'Which shape do you prefer? Why?'
'What do you prefer: to create ideas and work on exciting new concepts or to apply tried and tested approaches? Why?'

_____
_____
_____
_____

'Which shape do you prefer? Why?'
'What do you base your decisions on: facts or feelings?'
'What is more important to you: efficiency and profit or support and buy-in from everyone involved? Why?'

_____
_____
_____
_____

Shades

'Which color do you prefer? Why?'
'Where do you draw your energy - from inside you or what goes on around you? Why?'

_____
_____
_____

'Which color do you prefer? Why?'
'Do you prefer to leave everything to the last minute or plan your tasks way ahead? Why?'

_____
_____
_____

The T.W.I.S.T.T. Success Generator

Name _____ Date _____

Your influences: What you say, do, think and feel:

Sex

'Describe a situation, where you worked really success-fully with someone of the **same sex**. What was the secret of this success?'

'Describe a situation, where you worked with someone of the **same sex** and it didn't work out at all. Why did this happen?'

'Describe a situation, where you worked really success-fully with someone of the **opposite sex**. What was the secret of this success?'

'Describe a situation, where you were working with someone of the **opposite sex** and it didn't work out at all. Why did this happen?'

_____
_____
_____

Senses

'Tell me about your biggest success at work so far. Please try to recreate the scene in as much detail as possible for me. I'd like to be able to see what you saw, to hear what you heard and to understand how you felt.'

_____
_____

'Remember a situation where you had to deal with a difficult client/a challenging colleague. How did you deal with this situation? Describe in detail what you thought, did, said and felt.'

_____
_____

Status

'How much responsibility do you have at work (e.g. how many people report to you)?'

'What do you like about having/not having responsibility?'

_____
_____
_____

The T.W.I.S.T.T. Success Generator

Name _____   Date _____

Your influences: What you say, do, think and feel:

'Which country/countries had a significant influence on the way you think and act today? How would you describe this impact?'
'Where do you live now? How does this influence you?'

_____
_____
_____

'What sort of community do you live in?'
'What's good about it?'
'What could be better?'

_____
_____
_____

'When were you born?'
'How does your age affect your current feelings, actions and thoughts (e.g. did you think differently about a particular issue 10 years ago)?'

_____
_____
_____

'What do you do for a living?'
'How does your job affect your beliefs and behavior?'

_____
_____
_____

'What income bracket do you put yourself in: Low, medium or high?'
'How does your income affect your lifestyle?'

_____
_____
_____

The T.W.I.S.T.T. Success Generator

Name _____ Date _____

Your influences: What you say, do, think and feel:

'What religion or other beliefs do you have?'
'How does this affect your life?'

_____
_____
_____

'What language(s)/dialects do you speak?'
'How does this affect the way you communicate with others?'

_____
_____
_____

'What are the ethnic influences on you?'
'How do they affect your current lifestyle, feelings and actions?'

_____
_____
_____

'Who are the key influencers from your family and friends?'
'How do they influence you?'

_____
_____
_____

Social

A big reminder about the six *S*s

N.B.
The T.W.I.S.T.T. Success Generator
for team type targeting

- The T.W.I.S.T.T. Success Generator has been divided into sections. As you take people through the 'windows' in the T.W.I.S.T.T. all you have to do is tick the appropriate symbol – IN PENCIL. If people change their minds once you begin to discuss the implications of their choice then simply change the tick! For example, with SHAPES and SHADES we find that 75% of the time people agree with three or four out of the four sets. Sometimes, however, you have to change the lot.
- The key to the T.W.I.S.T.T., just like all the other psychological indicators, is that people feel comfortable with their description of them. Remember, this is only a fun way of establishing how best to 'turn your audience on' with the words, designs and colors they like. If it doesn't work then change your approach. Marketing people do it all the time!

What do I do with my T.W.I.S.T.T. results?

The T.W.I.S.T.T. has two main uses when targeting messages:

- targeting individuals
- targeting groups.

Match – targeting individuals

When targeting individuals, once you know what is their type the rest is easy. You simply have to develop your message with them in mind. You know, for example, that if they are a Triangle you must be short, sharp and to the point, the point being something about helping them make more money, profit, or a better career move.

Match – targeting groups

When targeting groups things get a bit more complicated. In fact this is why mass marketing is not particularly successful and individual targeting is. Try to appeal to everyone and you will appeal to no-one. However, what you can do is one of four things, in reverse order of effectiveness:

1   Try to appeal to them all by throwing everything in
2   Try to appeal to the biggest market with a more targeted message
3   Segment your market into sectors
4   Target them all individually.

What happens when you are forced to send out a missive to all 7,000 of your workforce, or even all seven of your team? What do you do? The chances of using the right language and finding the right hooks will be dependent on three key factors, your ability to watch, match and nudge and to segment your audience.

Now it's time to focus on the message

Having learned how to understand people, to recognize why they say what they say, now it is time to start tackling real issues. The way that works best, is not to 'shove' things at people. It is to ensure your messages fit their perceptions like a hand going into a glove. This is the power of rapport. It is all about matching what YOU have to say with the way THEY will best take it on board. This is the power of Watch, Match and Nudge'.

The final secret – of Nudge

Now that you know how to watch and match it is time to move things on a pace. You are ready for the third ring in our target. You're approaching the middle! This is where the old secret comes in:

'Let them think they thought of it themselves.'

This as good today as it ever was. We call it involvement. Not only will they think of it themselves, they will probably come up with a whole bunch of new ideas (from the Squiggles), detailed methods (from the Boxes), plans and actions (from the Triangles), and the best people to work on the teams to keep motivation high (from the Circles). So here is the final secret of Nudge.

What are their ideas on how they would go about tackling whatever it is you are trying to tackle? – so you can play this back to them as well.

Once you have THEIR ideas then you can put them together with YOUR ideas, and the whole thing becomes a joint effort. You don't of course have to do this with everything. Good strong leadership is as important to people as involvement and team work. It is now all a question of balance.

WHY Communicate? Making messages that work

The good thing for me is there are lots of good things about the WHY principle.

What we are going to cover now is how to get your messages across in a way that gives you a structure and format for whenever you are communicating. It is called 'WHY Communicate™'.

The good thing for you is that it is a surefire way of gaining immediate buy-in to whatever you have to say. You will get straight to people's hearts and minds and be able to generate the actions you need to help you succeed.

By following the principles of WHY Communicate™ you will be able to apply these principles to verbal communication, like speeches, presentations or even a telephone call. You will also be able to apply these to written communication – from a business journal, a report on strategy, to a memo or a poster for the notice board.

If you go back and look at the introduction in the three paragraphs above you will see the principle of WHY Communicate™. These three paragraphs have been written in the WHY Communicate™ format. This is a method that has been tried and tested on many people. They like it. It works. It is easy to apply.

Used as an introduction it is the 'attention grabber' that make people want to read on. Not all targeted copy needs to follow the exact order you are about to see in WHY Communicate™, but each of the elements will be involved if it is copy intended to do the following three things:

- get ATTENTION
- get BUY-IN
- get ACTION.

The WHY Communicate™ format comes straight from the advertising text book, which looks something like this.

> "*Lights, camera, action!*"

Create interest – e.g. in an advert on TV show an 'establishing shot' so that people know what to expect, or are 'surprised' into wanting more e.g. beach scene, enigmatic image.

Highlight the WIIFM – What's in it for me (the 'hook') e.g. enjoying delicious ice cream, drinking exotic new drink and attracting hordes of the opposite sex.

Show 'pack shot' – A picture of the product and brand name so that the next time they are in a purchasing mode they immediately think of and purchase Brand X and not Brand Y.

We are all experts at advertising, particularly at being on the receiving end! What we are not so good at is delivering. Here is your chance to generate some of the passion with your internal customers that the advertising agencies create with consumers.

Be your own advertising agency!
Write sexy copy!
Get promoted!

Does this sound like advertising hype? Oh well, at least WHY Communicate™ will make your memos more exciting!

> Would you like a
> taste of marketing?
> Nibble this!

We have been training the WHY Communicate™ principles for many years now, and have helped many thousands of people. Just like the promotional offer in the supermarket where you can try the piece of cheese to see if you like it, you can do the same with WHY Communicate™. It is simple, easy to remember and highly effective – and practice makes perfect.

Here it is again, the three principles of advertising when applied to writing or speaking;

1   **What** – get ATTENTION

2   **Hook** – get BUY-IN

3   **Your aim** – create the trigger to ACTION.

*W*hat

What do you want to talk about?

This is the topic of conversation. The overview only – NOT THE DETAIL. It is, in TV advertising, called the 'establishing shot'. At most you give them a short list of no more than three things you will cover.

*H*ook

What are the 'hooks' that will motivate them?

These are the personal benefits or WIIFMs; the What's In It For Me? Here you show how they can attain the things they have told you they want (you get this information from your research). This includes their personal 'hooks' like the need to be trained, developed, have a career, promotion, pay, leadership, future, security and to be involved and listened to.

*Y*our aim

What do you want them to think or do differently?

This is what YOU want to get out of it, or what YOU want them to do. Once you have established THEY want it, you can ask them to take action – but not the other way round!

Why why why why why (why not?)

An advertiser has somewhere between thirty seconds and one minute to get across the message, so do you.

The power of WHY Communicate™ comes in using the approach up front, at the beginning of any communication. Effective in printed material, it is even more powerful on screen. The essence of communication on computer screen, be it the Internet, Intranet or plain old e-mail is that brevity is the source of a hit!

There are instances where WHY Communicate™ is unnecessary, as in the case of instructions. However, if people have a CHOICE over whether they do or do not do something they move into a new mode – one of being a customer. This is when they need to know why they should do it and what is in it for them.

Hints and tips on writing WHY Communicate™

"
The good thing for you …
The good thing for you …
The good thing for you …
The good thing for you …
The good thing for you …
The good thing for you …
"

Opposite you'll see some of the words you can use in each of the three WHY Communicate™ sections. You will find that using these words saves you inventing your own. They are also tried and tested. Once you have got used to them then I would recommend you add some alternatives. Variety is the spice of life and it will keep your writing style fresh.

Clearly the 1, 2, 3 to WHY Communicate™

1   Clear introduction
2   Clear personal benefits or 'hooks'
3   Clear actions and results you want to achieve.

In the mental aerobics section at the end are your very own WHY pages to complete.

Phrases to use and build on when using WHY Communicate ™

*W*hat

Verbal   'What I would like to cover today is ...'
                'There are three hot topics I am going to address
                in this short slide presentation.'

Written   'This article is going to address a few key issues,
                these are ...'
                'The goals we have set ourselves are clear. This
                memo is about the two main issues we face in
                reaching these goals.'

The key here is to talk about 'it' – the subject matter.

*H*ook

Verbal   'You will be pleased to know that what you wanted
                has happened ...'
                'You have all said you would benefit from this hap-
                pening in a number of ways ...'

Written   'The good thing for you is ...'
or verbal   'You will be delighted to know'

The key here is to talk about 'you' – the target audience.

*Y*our aim

Verbal   'What I want to get from this meeting is.'
                'These are the actions I now want to happen'

Written   'The plans I want us to make will include ...'
                'I am asking that the project will now move for-
                ward by ...'

Now it's your turn to put WHY Communicate™ into practice.

Time to capture hearts and minds and deliver improved top and bottom line.

Then a final passionate KISS!

First it's time to ask

WHY...

**Mental aerobic exercise no. 15:
WHY Communicate by *e-mail***

What to do ...   Fill this out *before* you start the actual communication.

Hook for you ... If you get their 'hooks' and language right – success.

Your aim ...   The more you use WHY the more chance of success – GO FOR IT!

***W*hat**   (Up to three things I want you to know about '*it*')

1 _____

2 _____

3 _____

***H*ook**   (The good thing(s) for *you* is/are ...)

_____

_____

_____

***Y*our aim**   (What *I* want you to think/do/say)

_____

_____

_____

Mental aerobic exercise no. 16:
WHY Communicate *face to face*

What to do ...   Fill this out *before* you start the actual communication.

Hook for you ... If you get their 'hooks' and language right – success.

Your aim ...   The more you use WHY the more chance of success – GO FOR IT!

*W*hat   (Up to three things I want you to know about '*it*')

1 _____

2 _____

3 _____

*H*ook   (The good thing(s) for *you* is/are ...)

_____

_____

_____

*Y*our aim   (What *I* want you to think/do/say)

_____

_____

_____

Mental aerobic exercise no. 17:
WHY Communicate in a *speech*

What to do ...   Fill this out *before* you start the actual commu-
                  nication.

Hook for you ... If you get their 'hooks' and language right –
                  success.

Your aim ...   The more you use WHY the more chance of
                  success – GO FOR IT!

*W***hat**   (Up to three things I want you to know about *'it'*)

                  1 _____

                  2 _____

                  3 _____

*H***ook**   (The good thing(s) for *you* is/are ...)

                  _____

                  _____

                  _____

*Y***our aim**   (What *I* want you to think/do/say)

                  _____

                  _____

                  _____

Mental aerobic exercise no. 18:
WHY Communicate by *fax*

What to do ...   Fill this out *before* you start the actual communi-
                  cation.

Hook for you ... If you get their 'hooks' and language right –
                  success.

Your aim ...   The more you use WHY the more chance of
                  success – GO FOR IT!

***W*hat**   (Up to three things I want you to know about '*it*')

     1 _____

     2 _____

     3 _____

***H*ook**   (The good thing(s) for *you* is/are ...)

    _____

    _____

    _____

***Y*our aim**   (What *I* want you to think/do/say)

    _____

    _____

    _____

Mental aerobic exercise no. 19: WHY Communicate by *phone*

What to do ...   Fill this out *before* you start the actual communication.

Hook for you ... If you get their 'hooks' and language right – success.

Your aim ...   The more you use WHY the more chance of success – GO FOR IT!

*W*hat

(Up to three things I want you to know about '*it*')

1 _____

2 _____

3 _____

*H*ook

(The good thing(s) for *you* is/are ...)

_____

_____

_____

*Y*our aim

(What *I* want you to think/do/say)

_____

_____

_____

Mental aerobic exercise no. 20: WHY Communicate in a *document*

What to do ...   Fill this out *before* you start the actual communication.

Hook for you ... If you get their 'hooks' and language right – success.

Your aim ...   The more you use WHY the more chance of success – GO FOR IT!

***W*hat**   (Up to three things I want you to know about '*it*')

                  1 _____

                  2 _____

                  3 _____

***H*ook**   (The good thing(s) for *you* is/are ...)

                  _____

                  _____

                  _____

***Y*our aim**   (What *I* want you to think/do/say)

                  _____

                  _____

                  _____

You've done your best.

Now put it to the test.

What do your customers
think?

Do you have buy-in?

Time for a SWOTcheck™ ...

A final passionate KISS! – how to check your communication is working, the easy way

So there we have it, *Passion At Work*. Your motto for the future.

What's in it for me? **Don't TELL them – get them to BUY!**

This book has been all about getting people to buy. It has been about the two stages of getting buy-in. How?

- Understanding people and what motivates them
- Targeting your message.

BUT – and it is a BIG BUT – a word of warning! Marketing externally has been able to make some great claims about how successful the whole marketing process is. Yet it is worth remembering that for every successful product there are NINE failures. This may be nothing to do with the product. The marketing and advertising may have been exceptional. The trouble is, everyone else is producing exceptional products and advertising. There is a surplus of everything.

Competition is so intense these days that there are no guarantees of success any more.

One thing is sure. Marketing is a must. Understanding customers and meeting their needs is now the order of the day.

The same applies inside organizations. Too many programs of 'change' fail, not because of the competition, but because the internal marketing is nonexistent. There may be a promotional effort with a few posters and a video, but this is not marketing, it's promotion.

Programs of change fail because they fail to target internal customers.

They fail because the communication is often no better than a 5 out of 10.

Internal customers have their way of doing things, their own way of seeing the world, their needs, their wants, their desires. They need great internal marketing and communication from you. They deserve it. They have committed themselves to you. These internal customers are ready to buy from you. They do it from the external marketeers. When they do buy-in, the business benefits are tremendous.

Passion At Work has been about giving you the insights into the hearts and minds of your internal customers. Each and every one of them is a fascinating individual. Each and every one of them is working on a major lifetime project – themselves. If you want them to work on your projects you can't just pay them and tell them to get on with it any more. This new discipline of marketing internally is the way to achieve what you want by matching your business needs to your people's needs. This is plain old common sense. You can apply the principles personally through what we have learned with inter-relationship marketing. This is what the book has been about.

There is one question which now remains:

If I buy-in and action what is involved in creating Passion At Work, how will I know if it is working for me?

This is your ultimate WIIFM – Will Passion At Work give you measurable sustainable benefits?

This is the real test:

- Do you have buy-in?
- Have you captured hearts and minds?
- Have you improved top and bottom line?

And so to the bullseye. You'll only know you have buy-in if you ask what they now think, feel and believe. Our version of do-it-yourself marketing research is called SWOTcheck™.

BUY-IN – the way to check your results

How do you know if you have hit the target? Easy. Ask!

Here is a simple version of one of our Do It Yourself tools. This is a powerful research tool we call SWOTcheck™. It is modelled on the marketing tool called SWOT which stands for **S**trengths, **W**eaknesses, **O**pportunities and **T**hreats.

This simple version takes the SWOT concept and requires you to ask four simple questions. The exact words and order are important. For example if you just say to someone 'What do you think about how I communicate with you?' – be ready for a potential avalanche of some pretty negative comments like:

'Now you come to mention it I was really unhappy about …'

Neither you nor your interviewee will feel good.

SWOTcheck ™ – Here is what you do

- Tell the person you are looking for their feedback and would like 15 minutes of their time.
- Ask the four questions on the form.
- Fill out the scores as you finish each question.
- Ask why they have given you this score.
- Let them do the talking.
- Sit quietly and do not react to negative comments.
- Write down their responses legibly so you can read it later!
- Get them to agree that what you have written is what they said.
- Be ready to action what they say.

Now you have the feedback this is what marketing people do with a SWOT analysis.

Marketing Actions

Strengths – Build on them

Weakness – Work to reduce or eliminate it

Opportunities – Grab them!

Threats – Stamp on them before they stamp on you.

This simple tool will help you plan out what you need to do next when you have that all important feedback. By asking your customers for feedback you have already shown them you are interested and listening. However listening alone is not enough. By doing something about their feedback, you are beginning to apply the true marketing model – meeting customers needs. It is also the true Quality model – the goal is constant improvement.

You will also get some stunning innovations when you ask for their ideas or 'opportunities'. You'll soon find out what could stop people buying in to your ideas.

Now it's up to you. Be passionate about your customers – and guess what? They will be passionate about you.

SWOT a customer of yours

Use these forms to SWOT whatever you like e.g. a program, a piece of communication, a newsletter design. Have fun. Here's an example.

SWOTcheck™

Your comments	Your rating	Your reason for this rating
Please print	Fill in one arrow, e.g.	Please print

Strengths

What is good about

Our department ? — 1 2 3 4 ▷ ▷ ▶ ▷ Strong → Very strong

Why?

1	Friendly bunch	▷ ▷ ▷ ▶	1	Good on the phone
2	Hard working	▷ ▶ ▷ ▷	2	Stay late
3	Good quality	▷ ▷ ▶ ▷	3	Meet our needs

Weaknesses

What could be better about

Our department ? Weak → Very weak

Why?

1	Faster response	▷ ▷ ▷ ▶	1	Always late
2	Bureaucratic	▷ ▶ ▷ ▷	2	Too many forms
3	____	▷ ▷ ▷ ▷	3	____

Opportunities

What ideas do you have on

Our department ? Good idea → Very good

Why?

1	New software	▷ ▷ ▷ ▶	1	Better systems
2	____	▷ ▷ ▷ ▷	2	____
3	____	▷ ▷ ▷ ▷	3	____

Threats

What would stop you dealing with

Our department ? Threat → Very strong threat

Why?

1	New supplier	▷ ▷ ▷ ▶	1	Seen a good one
2	Slow response	▷ ▷ ▶ ▷	2	Affects us too
3	____	▷ ▷ ▷ ▷	3	____

SWOTcheck™

Your comments	**Your rating**	**Your reason for this rating**
Please print	Fill in one arrow, e.g.	Please print

Strengths

What is good about

1 2 3 4
▷ ▷ ▶ ▷
Strong ⟶ Very strong

.... ?

1 _____	▷ ▷ ▷ ▷	1 _____
2 _____	▷ ▷ ▷ ▷	2 _____
3 _____	▷ ▷ ▷ ▷	3 _____

Why?

Weaknesses

What could be better about

.... ?   Weak ⟶ Very weak

1 _____	▷ ▷ ▷ ▷	1 _____
2 _____	▷ ▷ ▷ ▷	2 _____
3 _____	▷ ▷ ▷ ▷	3 _____

Why?

Opportunities

What ideas do you have on

.... ?   Good idea ⟶ Very good

1 _____	▷ ▷ ▷ ▷	1 _____
2 _____	▷ ▷ ▷ ▷	2 _____
3 _____	▷ ▷ ▷ ▷	3 _____

Why?

Threats

What would stop you dealing with

.... ?   Threat ⟶ Very strong threat

1 _____	▷ ▷ ▷ ▷	1 _____
2 _____	▷ ▷ ▷ ▷	2 _____
3 _____	▷ ▷ ▷ ▷	3 _____

Why?

SWOTcheck™

Your comments	Your rating	Your reason for this rating
Please print	Fill in one arrow, e.g.	Please print

Strengths

What is good about

.... ?

1 2 3 4
▷ ▷ ▶ ▷
Strong ⟶ Very strong

Why?

1 _____   ▷ ▷ ▷ ▷   1 _____

2 _____   ▷ ▷ ▷ ▷   2 _____

3 _____   ▷ ▷ ▷ ▷   3 _____

Weaknesses

What could be better about

.... ?

Weak ⟶ Very weak

Why?

1 _____   ▷ ▷ ▷ ▷   1 _____

2 _____   ▷ ▷ ▷ ▷   2 _____

3 _____   ▷ ▷ ▷ ▷   3 _____

Opportunities

What ideas do you have on

.... ?

Good idea ⟶ Very good

Why?

1 _____   ▷ ▷ ▷ ▷   1 _____

2 _____   ▷ ▷ ▷ ▷   2 _____

3 _____   ▷ ▷ ▷ ▷   3 _____

Threats

What would stop you dealing with

.... ?

Threat ⟶ Very strong threat

Why?

1 _____   ▷ ▷ ▷ ▷   1 _____

2 _____   ▷ ▷ ▷ ▷   2 _____

3 _____   ▷ ▷ ▷ ▷   3 _____

Have fun researching, targeting, responding to your customers needs; have fun and success with Passion At Work.

And in the great tradition of researching and getting feedback, here is our address, e-mail and Website. Tell us what's good, what could be better, what opportunities you or we could have, what's stopping you using the processes and tools.

The good thing for you is you'll find lots of interesting things and people on our Website – and you'll be bang up to date with how to get Passion At Work.

What I would be passionate about is hearing from you. Thanks in advance.

MCA
Court Garden House
Pound Lane
Marlow
Bucks SL7 2AE
UK
Tel: +44(0) 1628 473217
Fax: +44(0) 1628 474011
Email: kthomson@mca.source.co.uk
Website: www.mca-group.com

DEEPER PASSION AT WORK!

The Goforit List

If you want to get deeper into Passion At Work then I have listed the people below against each section in the book; with the odd book reference. Look them up. There is a lot of great work around each of the sections. Have fun.

Shapes – Try the *Career Tracks* videos or courses on what they have called Psycho Geometrics – Shapes to you and me. Great video.

Shades – Read the *Luscher Colour Test* (with free color swatches to play with when doing your test) – Washington Square (Boxy?) Press. Great for parties, although you are not supposed to!

Shapes and Shades together – Devour anything on Myers Briggs – go on the course; get qualified in it – I did. Tough test to allow you to administer the Myers Briggs Type Indicator MBTI, but worth the hard work.

Sex – Anything by Deborah Tannen, like *You just don't understand* or by John Gray like *Men are from Mars, Women are from Venus*. There is also a lot of other gender-based psychology books around. I know I've read them to research this book, and because some are, well, you know ... so REVEALING!

Senses – I can't begin to list the books or workshops on NLP – Neuro Linguistic Programming. Start with Richard Bandler (a co-founder) and Paul McKenna (the famous hypnotist) – these two trained me, so now I'm a qualified 'practitioner'. Great course, if you can stand the colorful language!!

Status –

- **At home** – *I'm OK, You're OK* is an OK book developed on Dr Eric Bernes' theories and popularized by Thomas Harris in this, and the *Staying OK* book (Pan). There are a number of other books on Transactional Analysis. Oh, and if you want to go really deep, get Freud, Jung (see also Myers Briggs) and oh, throw in some Scott Peck, with a dash of Celestine prophecy for other psychology type stuff.
- **At work** – From Taylor to Hertzberg, from Maslow to Blanchard. Go grab any management books on or by the 'gurus' to check out Status at work. There is a century's worth of reading!

Social/Economic – I can't begin to list all the marketing books. Yes I can – start with the latest edition of *Principles of Marketing* by Philip Kotler. THE handbook on all these marketing principles and practices. Next try the libraries or book shops, or try the UK-based Chartered Institute of Marketing or American Marketing Association for courses, etc.

The Passion Pack – And all the other concepts rolled into one: call us at MCA (+44) 1628 473217, at our UK riverside headquarters in Marlow-on-Thames, or visit our Web site at www.mca-group.com

Thanks for your passion. Until the follow ups …

INDEX